FIXING
POSITIONS

FIXING
POSITIONS

FIXING POSITIONS

Trailer Sailing the West

MATTS G. DJOS

S

Sheridan House

First published 2008 by
Sheridan House Inc.
145 Palisade Street
Dobbs Ferry, NY 10522
www.sheridanhouse.com

While all reasonable care has been taken in the publication of this book, the publisher takes no responsibility for the use of the methods or products described in the book.

Library of Congress Cataloging-in-Publication Data

Djos, Matts G.
    Fixing positions : trailer sailing the west / Matts G. Djos.
        p. cm.
    Includes bibliographical references and index.
    ISBN 978-1-57409-268-4 (pbk. : alk. paper)
    1. Sailing—North America—Guidebooks. I. Title.
    GV811.D57 2008
    797.124097—dc22   2008034614

ISBN 978 1 57409 268 4

Edited by Dieter Loibner
Designed by Keata Brewer

Printed in the United States of America

To my wife Jeanine,
my beloved, my soul mate, my shipmate;
and to my daughters Heidi, Joanna, and Monika,
remarkable women all!

Contents

Appendices

List of Maps

Preface

The Kaleidoscope of Change

In 1976, we left the Pacific Northwest and moved to western Colorado to begin a new life in the high country of the Rocky Mountains. The scenery was majestic and the skiing terrific, which made us feel good, but it wasn't long before we began to miss Puget Sound and a chance to go sailing.

We just had to have a boat, a simple little yacht, light and forgiving, easy to haul and launch. We searched the local marinas and the nickel ads until we chanced on a little-used 15-foot Chrysler Man O'War dinghy that was about as stable as a bud vase. At the time, she seemed perfect: pretty under sail, easy to set up and launch, and fast. We bought her on the spot, towed her home, decked her out with a racing stripe and replaced the mainsail. For the following few years we hitched her to the family sedan and had a grand time sailing the lakes of the Colorado high country.

Of course, I had much to learn, and there were moments when I tempted fate. But those moments served as a valuable reality check, offering a solid perspective for pursuing the greater horizon. I once thought I could defy an approaching high-country thunderstorm by sailing through a katabatic gale to reach the dock. It was a fascinating challenge but a stupid idea. Halfway down the lake, the gale caught up to us and smacked the boat with such terrifying power that we suddenly plowed through the water like a jet ski in a waterspout. Of course, this was too much for our little vessel, which wobbled out of control as the rudder popped to the surface. Suddenly the boat turned toward land and attacked the nearest beach. We took a hard hit. As the boat lurched over the sand I scrambled up the windward rail, desperately trying to secure the sail before the howling wind could flog it to shreds.

Afterwards, I checked hull and centerboard for damage and was astonished to discover that, except for a couple of scratches, they were fully intact, proof that small boats can also be amazingly durable and very forgiving. Later I discovered that larger rigs are not nearly as kind or forgiving and are at higher risk of sustaining a good deal of damage when things go wrong.

Of course, from that moment on I wasn't so sure of my own durability. Regardless of whether my boat was up to such antics, I concluded that I was not. After capsizing a few times during later outings and sampling the chill waters of the Colorado high country, I realized that, fun aside, I'd better find a safer option, something a bit larger, a bit more stable, and quite a bit less tippy.

I suppose it was a matter of fate or luck, but it wasn't long before Jeanine and I discovered an abused Victoria 18 in a used-car lot. A cat had taken up residence inside and the boat was speckled with mud and bird droppings. Yet, despite all the dirt and oxidation, she appeared sound. And she looked like she was also going to be a good deal safer than the Man O'War. And so KAPRICE joined our family's sailing armada. We painted her bottom, bought a 6-hp outboard and a new mainsail, declared her lovely and went sailing. We towed her off to Ridgway Reservoir, Ruedi Reservoir, Blue Mesa Reservoir, and Lake Vallecito high in the San Juan Mountains, which had special appeal. Three 13,000-foot peaks towered over the lake's emerald waters like stone sentinels; and a 10-15-knot wind usually sprang up at 11:00 a.m. and died promptly at 7:00 p.m. Sometimes, especially in late afternoon, the thunder rolled down through the canyons and valleys, the wind freshened and churned up the lake. I had experienced enough mountain storms with the Man O'War to know that being safe meant turning tails. We always doused our sails and headed for camp at the first sign of an impending gale. KAPRICE on the other hand, was safe enough to ride out the storm at her anchor. The rain sounded lovely as it beat against our tent and we lay safely beneath the canvas smelling the pines and marveling at the power and mystery of this high-country paradise.

We trailered KAPRICE farther and farther from home and once managed to get lost in one of the canyons of Lake Powell. We had pitched camp in a pristine cove on Halls Creek Bay, about 10 miles from the launch ramp at Bullfrog Marina, but KAPRICE was too small to transport us, our two daughters, Heidi and Joanna, and all of our gear in one trip. Therefore, we had to make two runs, but as Jeanine and I headed back out to camp on the second trip, the sun disappeared beneath the horizon when we were halfway across the bay, and the sky suddenly turned pitch black beneath a sinister blanket of clouds.

We tried to find the channel, but it seemed like it had disappeared in the darkness. We knew that it was near Buoy 93,

The Victoria 18 KAPRICE

but that seemed to be gone too! We dug our flashlights and searched the canyon for some kind of entry until an opening of sorts loomed ahead. I turned up that channel while Jeanine scoured the surrounding walls with the beam of her flashlight to help us find our way. Suddenly, she shrieked in horror. Hundreds of flapping, squeaking bats had emerged from a nearby cave and were flitting and diving around our running lights, which had attracted hordes of flying bugs. Jeanine is not a big fan of bats (there's something about them getting tangled in her hair), but she bit her lip, ignored the tiny beasts and continued to shine her light against the sandstone, which seemed to twist this and that way with no recognizable pattern or direction.

This, we realized, was not the right channel. We were poking around Lost Eden Canyon or in one of the side channels, but most certainly we were lost in Lost Eden. I didn't know where I could turn back, but I knew that we had to find some way to get back to our camp at Halls Creek Bay.

Just when all seemed hopeless, a brilliant full moon peeked over the horizon, illuminating the canyon walls in a pale blue light, and pointing the way out of Eden. Gladly, I pushed the throttle all the way forward, and we motored out of this maze, passing Buoy 93, which materialized exactly and miraculously where it should have been all along, and returning to our campsite, where we found the girls hunkered down, peering out into the spooky darkness, waiting for the tell-tale sound of our engine. Once we had entered the correct channel, finding our daughters was easy, because they had stoked the campfire, which was the beacon that pointed the way.

That night, after an excited reunion, we realized that we

had discovered our own Eden, found our way to freedom and learned about our precarious circumstances in the great scheme of things. On a more practical level, we recognized the importance of timing the sunset correctly, the dangers of navigating unfamiliar places in the dark, and the need to allow a sufficient margin of safety when planning a trip.

Equipped with this wisdom we expanded our trailer trips to new venues, including Washington and California. But after getting beat up in a desert storm on Lake Powell, we realized that a boat like KAPRICE wouldn't suffice if we were going to do any extended cruising. We were ready for a boat that was a little bigger, a little more comfortable, and a good deal more substantial. We drove to Denver, stopped at just about every large marina in town and settled on a moderately priced MacGregor 22, which came with a pretty good engine, a full set of sails, and a host of extras, including tools, ground tackle, and electronics. We took the boat for a test run, closed the sale, and brought her home for a quick refit, a new paint job and a shakedown. After the christening ceremony, AL-LEGRA and her crew were ready to explore the inland waters of New Mexico, Nevada, and Utah. Lake Powell remained our first love, because of its spectacular surroundings and challenging winds and because it offered pristine beauty and solitude. By the end of our second summer, we had explored most of the lake's middle channel, marveled at the beauty of Moki, Slick Rock, and Iceberg canyons, sailed the Great Bend, and camped the distant reaches of Good Hope Bay at the north end.

But soon we stumbled upon an advertisement for a Balboa 26. We knew that she had been one of the largest trailerable sailboats of her time, and we drove to Denver for a closer look. It was love at first sight. The boat was pristine and we bought her without so much as a shakedown cruise, refitted her, and named her LADY JEANINE. We did not realize at the time, but we were well into an unforgettable 15-year trailer boat odyssey. With the Man O'War, KAPRICE and ALLEGRA already behind us, each boat, each venue, each highway, and each voyage was the start of a fresh adventure whose full significance would be almost impossible to grasp until years later.

During the next few summers, we trailered LADY JEANINE to Lake Powell as much as we did with ALLEGRA, only this time we explored the farthest navigable reaches of the San Juan wilderness, the Grand Staircase-Escalante National Monument, Wahweap Bay and Padre Bay far to the south. By the summer of 1998, we had gained enough confidence to think about trying our hand at coastal sailing, so we trailered LADY JEANINE over 1,200 miles to our former home state of Washington and cruised the Saratoga Passage and the San Juan Islands. The following year, we returned and spent more than a month on the northern Puget Sound and the east coast of Vancouver Island in Canada.

In 2000, we expanded our horizon to include ocean sailing on the California coast. We trailered the Balboa over 850 miles to explore Southern California and the following year we refined our bluewater skills cruising in the Channel Islands south of Santa Barbara. When I was granted a year's sabbatical by my employer, we took LADY JEANINE south of the border to sail the Gulf of California.

We had come a long way since those early years with the Man O'War in the high country of Colorado. We had certainly expanded our horizons, our skills, and our appreciation for the beauty and the challenges of distant venues. Each new voyage brought new trials, new encounters, and new perspectives seen through the kaleidoscope of change. Yet, even as we ranged farther afield, it became clear that our odyssey was only in its infancy. There was so much more to learn, so much that we had yet to experience. All we had to do was search out the distant sea and hoist sail.

Part I

Lake Powell

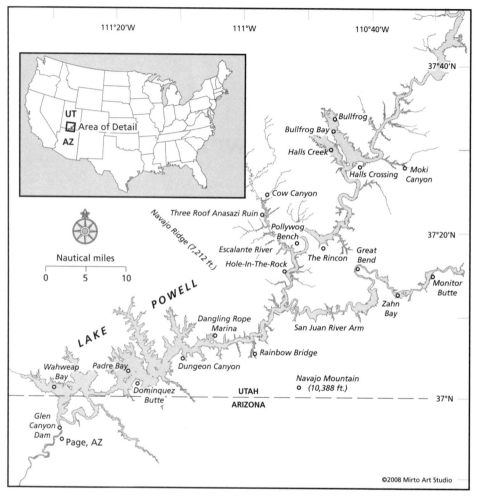

Map of Lake Powell

Ancient Rocks
and Ancient Wonders

More than 35 million years ago, when dinosaurs dominated life on earth and the giant cleft of the Grand Canyon had barely begun to form, rivers sculpted a fantastic labyrinth of canyons and arroyos on the Colorado Plateau during their inexorable westward journey to the sea. Today, innumerable vestiges of this age are inscribed in the spectacular canyon walls and palisades of the Escalante, the San Juan, and the Colorado rivers where they have been dammed up to form the 180-mile-long Lake Powell. While their paths have changed over time, they still converge within miles of each other in what is now the watershed of the Escalante Rim and 10,388-foot Navajo Mountain. This is one of the most unique and spectacular boating venues on the North American continent. And for sailors with a passion for solitude, warm desert breezes, and breathtaking scenery, it could prove to be the experience of a lifetime. In the summer of 1994 we trailered ALLEGRA, our MacGregor 22

some 230 miles from our home in Grand Junction to Bullfrog Marina on Lake Powell, where we planned to explore
the canyons and arroyos of the Colorado River just north of
the Escalante confluence.

The southwest desert of eastern Utah is Big Sky country,
a solitary wilderness of gold, vermillion, and blue, with very
few truck stops and hardly a mailbox or utility pole to pierce
the horizon. As we turned off I-70 west of Green River and
drove through tiny Hanksville, once the hideout of outlaws
Butch Cassidy and the Sundance Kid, a series of imposing
peaks trailed off to the west, while canyons of the desert
stretched far to the south. But we kept going, towing the
McGregor across a solitary mesa and a series of arroyos until
we ascended the Henry Mountains and the glittering waters
of the lake came into view, an emerald paradise that extended
nearly to the great portal of the Grand Canyon itself. Jeanine
touched my hand, roused our daughters, Joanna and Heidi,
from their magazines, and pointed to a small marina far below
us—our destination. We could hardly wait.

We arrived at Bullfrog just before noon, readied and
launched ALLEGRA, locked truck and trailer, cut our lines and
took course across Bullfrog Bay. As we watched the marina
fade in our wake we all grinned with anticipation—our adventure had begun. Our ancient 9.9-hp Johnson pushed us along
at ¾-throttle, while I put up my feet on the port bench and
secured the tiller with a loose double wrap. Skirting a series of
canyons and palisades, we made our way past Iceberg
Canyon, a long gorge of steep cliffs with six secluded side
canyons, and turned southwest at the Rincon, the former
riverbed of the Colorado, which is now dry and abandoned.
Beyond the Rincon we passed beneath a series of battlements,
which sit on top of palisades that towered at least a thousand

ALLEGRA, a McGregor Venture, is secured to an improvised
Med-moor. The stern is close enough to a shallow underwater
shelf allowing easy offloading and access

feet above us. Rounding the last of the cliffs, four massive
rainbow amphitheaters came into view.

During summer and fall, good sailing on Lake Powell can
be found near a high ridge or mountain just west or southwest of the main channel. These barriers cool the westerlies
when they rise over the summits and as the air continues to
move eastward, it rapidly descends to the lake, sometimes in
gusts that can exceed 30 knots. The principle works like an
offshore breeze, except that the jagged terrain of the desert
makes these winds unpredictable, as they refract and change
direction rapidly, sometimes by as much as 90 degrees. In
some locations, where the surrounding palisades are high and
steep, the wind may even disappear, which can be frustrating
for purists who cruise the lake under sail alone. We continued

15

Securing the stern mooring line by wrapping it around a massive sandstone boulder toward the confluence of the Colorado and Escalante Rivers near Buoy 70—the buoys on Lake Powell are numbered more or less according to their distance from Glen Canyon Dam— and decided to put in near Pollywog Bench. (A bench in the geological sense is a level area on the flank of a hill, ridge, or mountain.) The channel here offers excellent sailing and has some beautiful and protected east-facing coves, so we would be well sheltered from any storms.

Our own private cove for the night was fed by an artesian stream that meandered through a tiny natural garden at the far end and also had a high sandstone brow that shielded the mast from lightning. The shoreline was terraced with sandstone shelves and tables while to the southwest Navajo Ridge rose more than 7,000 feet above the lake. Directly overhead, three mysterious Anasazi circles had been carved into the sandstone. Later, during a short hike, we discovered an Anasazi granary just beneath a small amphitheater.

We backed into the cove and anchored Mediterranean style stern-to-shore after setting a bow anchor. Our Danforth clawed into the mud that was washed down by the artesian stream as I put the engine in full reverse to make sure it was properly set. Once I was satisfied, I also deployed a stern line and a second anchor and I set out a couple of fenders to protect ALLEGRA against the rocky shoreline, our private "Pleistocene dock," no more than a foot away. Preparing for a dinner ashore, we first offloaded our cooking gear, the bimini and the table and then hiked to a vantage point overlooking the main channel. The afternoon winds played softly on the lake surface and the afternoon sun created a spectacular display of red, gold, and violet on the west-facing walls. The steep canyon rim just behind us descended to the lake in a succession of natural arches and directly across the channel, a 1,500-foot palisade towered above the river like a primeval sentry.

As we made our way back to ALLEGRA, we first could smell it: the pungent odor of cat musk. Then we saw it: Just to the left of the trail, a fresh set of cougar tracks led toward a small amphitheater directly behind us. "Here, kitty-kitty," whispered Jeanine as we accelerated our pace on the way back to the boat. Cougars have little interest in human contact, but there have been incidents. I suppose it wasn't much of a deterrence (such a cat can easily jump more than 20 feet), but we moved the boat away from the shoreline and reset the anchors anyway. "There," I said with a grin, trying to comfort the rest of the family. "We'd certainly hear something when he jumps and lands on the cabin top." They were not impressed.

After a quiet night, a ten-to fifteen-knot breeze started to fill in around 11 a.m. on the following day. Time to weigh anchor and set sail. As ALLEGRA headed out into the main channel, I dropped and bolted the keel, hoisted the main and killed the engine. When we raised the genoa it flogged wildly for an instant, but we got it under control quickly as Jeanine, who was at the helm, fell off to a course due south, toward a series of cascading fissures. As we closed on the confluence of the Escalante the wind shifted, following the southward curve of the main channel. By the time we passed Buoy 68, we carried too much canvas for sailing closehauled, so we eased off. Heading down the main channel, a series of powerful gusts struck our little yacht, threatening to knock us flat, but each time we corrected by "feathering" the helm, luffing quickly to blunt the force of the initial strike. Then we fell off again to steady the boat and pick up some speed. The larger waves broke over the bow and doused our double berth beneath the open pop-top. Elsewhere this would have been a major nuisance, but not here in desert country, where it was hot and dry, so the soaked cushions and blankets dried quickly.

At Buoy 67 we turned south, toward a lovely little bay that lies beneath the famous "Hole-in-the-Rock," a sheer, U-shaped crevice. In 1879, the Mormon San Juan mission passed through here, rough-locking the axles of their horse- and ox-drawn wagons with chains, so they could lower them to the canyon floor, over a thousand feet below.

It was getting late in the day, so we brought ALLEGRA around for a downwind run back to our cove. She sometimes wallowed when she ran wing-and-wing, so we hardened up a little and steered the boat on a series of deep reaches for better pressure and a more responsive helm. The speedometer showed a consistent six knots, getting close to seven once in a while. Even though we made good time, this was still the leisure part of the trip. I spread out some cushions, the girls put on a couple of our favorite sailing tapes and we enjoyed the sensation of our little boat dancing with the wind.

The canyon walls shimmered against the desert varnish. We passed a sandy beach that ended in a reef, a hidden cove and a cottonwood bower. Near Buoy 68, we passed a tiny arroyo and glimpsed the characteristic shape of a honey pot dome. As we reached our cove, the sun was beginning to dip behind Pollywog Bench. The resident ravens and chipmunks scattered in all directions as we motored in to tie up for the night. Later, after a quick dip in the cove, we fired up the barbecue for some hamburgers that were accompanied by Jeanine's crispy salads and followed by a bowl of pineapple, clementine and apple. After the meal we watched carps come to the shoreline to compete with the ravens for the leftovers. Just as we finished, a full moon rose over the sandstone cliffs to the east accompanied by the twinkling of the evening star.

To cool down before turning in we took another dip in the crystalline waters. After a long day on the water that was capped by a fine meal, Jeanine and the girls fell asleep almost instantly, their breathing in perfect harmony with the motion of the boat and the sound of the waves lapping against the hull. We'd come to Lake Powell for the peace and beauty of the high desert, and already had fallen under the spell of our surroundings.

The following day, we headed north in a steady 15-knot southwesterly trying to stay in the shade cast by the mainsail on both gybes as we sailed past magnificent buttes and arroyos and marveled at a massive amphitheater with sheer walls that plunged more than 250 feet into the depths of the lake. Making port for the night, I tied off ALLEGRA between two rock outcroppings, welcomed by the echoes of birdsong, while directly above our anchorage, we could see a natural garden of maidenhair ferns, blue columbine, and tiny shrubs that were fed by an artesian spring. We swam ashore, and clambered over a rock fall to take a last look at the channel. But a surprise awaited us when we got back on the boat: A rather large water snake had somehow managed to slither aboard and had made her home in ALLEGRA's keel well. Of course, the girls would have none of it, so I spent the next half hour trying to motivate our uninvited guest to leave, while the crew anxiously awaited the resolution of this stowaway affair. The snake didn't insist on our company, as it turned out and, after some encouragement, slipped over the side, wrig-

LADY JEANINE under sail in a light breeze just north of the Rincon on Lake Powell

gled ashore, and disappeared beneath some maidenhair ferns. Paradise, as it turned out, still has snakes.

The following morning, as ALLEGRA swung lazily at her moorings, we feasted on blueberry pancakes accompanied by a Chopin piano concerto on the stereo and the plaintiff cries of a canyon wren coming from the cove behind us. The beauty of this moment nearly overwhelmed Jeanine and me. "Can't these moments last forever?" she asked, choking back tears. Lake Powell had worked its magic. Here in its narrow canyons and broad amphitheaters lay a sanctuary where life could be savored at a leisurely pace, solitude seemed infinite, and beauty was sublime.

That night we swam in the moonlight and slept on deck, under the rioting stars. The following day, we returned to Bullfrog to conclude this trip. But there would be plenty more such odysseys. The possibilities were endless. Perhaps we'd explore the upper reaches of the Escalante or the San Juan. Or we'd head south to Dangling Rope or Rainbow Arch. There would be plenty of choices, but one thing was certain: There was plenty of time for desert sailing ahead.

And indeed there was time, so much of it that our sailing prospects grew like desert flowers. Time and again we revisited Lake Powell, explored its majestic canyons, anchored beneath majestic amphitheaters, and weathered lightning and sand storms. One day we came across a well kept and little used Balboa 26 that was to become LADY JEANINE, our next vessel. She was in pristine condition, a floating palace compared to ALLEGRA, our trusted companion. She was safer, especially when we had to weather the fury of desert storms. She could carry two or three weeks worth of provisions, and the cockpit was large enough for a civilized dinner on board, so we no longer had to spend an afternoon lugging tables, coolers, and cookware ashore. And so we bought her and refitted her and used her to expand our cruising horizons to include just about every canyon and tributary in the Glen Canyon Recreation Area. We spent the following spring planning a Lake Powell itinerary that included a month-long excursion to the western and easternmost reaches of the San Juan and Escalante Rivers. We could hardly wait to get under way.

Desert Storms

The American desert is notorious for sudden, violent storms, and nowhere is this more evident than at Lake Powell. For Jeanine and me, two storms in particular are engraved in our memory, perhaps because they took the full measure of us—we were tested by the sudden, awesome power of the Southwest weather and wilderness—and they made us just a bit wiser and a bit more circumspect.

We had set up camp in Moki Canyon about ten miles north of Bullfrog and had enjoyed three beautiful warm, sunny days when NOAA issued a weather alert: a low-pressure system was moving in fast from the southwest, and we could expect gale force winds sometime before midnight. We knew that the canyons of Lake Powell sometimes generate a venturi or compression effect that could wreak havoc during major windstorms; and we rummaged the boat for extra chain, extra mooring lines, and the two spare anchors. We then secured the boat with a scattering of lines and hawsers, and buried all of the anchors under a pile of boulders and rubble.

Shortly after 10 p.m., a slight wind refracted off the far wall, and less than a half hour later it had increased to a howl and tore through the canyon pounding the boat in a deluge of rain and sand. As the wind ripped our camp ashore, it turned cold—extremely cold. ALLEGRA, our trusted MacGregor 22, bolted to port and starboard and strained against her moorings. The flying sand, the mist, and the pounding rain penetrated every nook and cranny on the boat. For the next two hours, we jerked and bumped and rocked with every gust while huddled below deck, condemned to endure nature's fury.

I became increasingly concerned about ALLEGRA breaking free from her moorings, even though she was secured by six different lines and four anchors. After a violent blast that thrust the boat sideways until it bounced off the beach, I shoved open the hatch, peered into the howling, sand-filled darkness, and trained the flashlight on a tangle of lines and anchors. They were tight as violin strings, but appeared secure. Shortly after midnight, the storm suddenly subsided and the canyon turned dead silent. The water calmed and lapped softly at our transom, while a crescent moon peeked over the battlement to the east. But our shore camp bore the signs of destruction. The tent had been flattened, bimini, tables, and chairs were buried in the sand, while other camping gear was scattered along the shoreline amidst broken branches. Later we learned that we had been battered by 70-knot gusts, that a catamaran had cartwheeled up the beach at Bullfrog and that a trailer had been flipped on its side.

A year later, we were tested again as we motored down the main channel just south of Lake Canyon, one dark August afternoon. But that time it was worse. NOAA radio issued a weather alert: Within the hour, a thunderstorm was expected to hit Page, Arizona, and all boaters and campers in the vicinity of Wahweap Bay were advised to move to higher ground and seek shelter. Since we were some seventy miles north, we saw no cause for alarm. We took the alert as an advisory and continued on our course.

Parts of Lake Powell are bordered by towering battlements that shorten the horizon, especially in the vicinity of Halls Creek Marina and Slick Rock Canyon, where it is almost impossible to see approaching storm cells until they are directly overhead.

As we approached Lake Canyon, the sun disappeared behind a blanket of thick, gray clouds and it began to look like we might be caught in a rainstorm. Perhaps, we thought, it was a remnant of the weather that had hit Page. But what struck twenty minutes later was unlike anything we could have possibly expected.

As we passed Buoy 87, we were overwhelmed by torrential rain and hail that struck in a series of microbursts, turning the channel into a maelstrom of spindrifts and waterspouts. As we pounded headlong into breaking waves, the scuppers were overwhelmed and it felt like half the channel was being tossed into the cockpit. Suddenly, the canyon walls exploded with a series of flashflood waterfalls that shot over the battlements in a hail of spray and mist and plunged more than a thousand feet to the lake below. They were beautiful but deadly, and I fought to keep clear of them, holding my course in the center of the channel, although this increased our exposure to lightning.

When a loose channel buoy passed behind us I decided that I had seen enough. I swung the boat around to head north toward Halls Creek Marina, running with the wind and the waves, the engine at full throttle. Engulfed by spindrift, ALLEGRA surfed the waves while lightning struck in such close proximity that I could smell the ozone. We were caught in mid-channel with steep cliffs on either side, some five miles away from the nearest cove that offered shelter. Dodging lighting that struck the battlements around us, we scurried north, cutting through the mist of the waterfalls that blanketed the channel in a steamy haze.

We passed another itinerant buoy that had washed against a rock. The VHF reported a number of houseboats that were on the hard after they'd broken loose from their moorings at Bullfrog Bay. Later we heard of bass boats that got swamped and sank, leaving their occupants stranded.

Wet, wretchedly cold and numb, I decided that our best option was to crank up the keel, and put ALLEGRA on the beach in a shallow cove in Halls Creek Bay. At the entry channel we turned broadside to the wind and motored west, parallel to the beach until we found a small refuge at the far end of the bay. I quickly raised the keel, gunned the engine, and made straight for the shore. ALLEGRA slammed into the sand and slid up the beach. Jeanine and I jumped clear, mooring lines and anchors in hand. We secured the boat with two stern lines and tied two more around a couple of boulders while lightning flashed everywhere and rain pelted us mercilessly.

Because I was concerned about the mast and the risk of a lightning strike, and I remembered a story about a houseboat that suffered a direct hit that killed everyone aboard, I thought it better to take our chances ashore until the storm had passed. So we sat on the beach for about ten minutes, surrounded by lightning and got soaked to the skin. Then a kangaroo rat scurried past Jeanine—and then another. "That's enough," she announced. She had no patience with jumping rodents, even if they showed no interest in her and just looked for shelter from the rain. Preferring lightning to rats, she got up, marched over to the boat, climbed back aboard and down into the cabin, where it was dry and clear of rats. I was getting fed up too, and followed her example.

Soon the storm moved on and the countryside was peaceful again. One might never have guessed that just a few moments ago our world had been turned upside down, except for the dark patina on the canyon walls, some beach erosion and some fresh gulleys and washes. From that day on, we never traversed Glen Canyon without carefully checking the sky. At the smallest sign of a cumulonimbus or thunderhead clouds to the southwest, we preferred to stay put. The weather on Lake Powell, we realized, is capable of sudden, terrifying storms that can be accompanied by waterspouts, flash floods and waterfalls, lightning and three- to five-foot waves with steep crests and narrow troughs that can swamp the hardiest of vessels. Our own experience reminded us that we too can be surprised and humbled when we overreach and test our luck.

A Farther Range

While Joanna and Heidi couldn't accompany us, one of our most memorable cruises aboard LADY JEANINE, our Balboa 26, was our exploration of the far reaches of the Escalante River and the easternmost navigable reaches of the San Juan River. We planned to depart Bullfrog in mid-June, motor south to the confluence of these two rivers and push upriver as far as possible. To re-provision we planned to return to Page, and work our way back north to explore the last navigable portion of the Escalante arm.

On the lower San Juan we motored past spectacular oases, forest hideaways, and immense rainbow amphitheaters until, about ten miles upriver, we broke out of the canyon labyrinth and entered a large bay with a shoreline that was punctuated by a series of massive rock falls. Within minutes, a fresh breeze tumbled down Navajo Mountain so we killed the engine, set sail and ran east with a sweet following breeze. Under the Navajo's summit glimmered a tiny patch of snow, shrinking in the merciless heat of the desert sun, while to the north, a long, unbroken, rust-colored ridge towered 2,000 feet above the surface of the bay.

We ran the full length of the reserve, decided it was the perfect sanctuary for the night, and dropped anchor in a secluded cove beneath the battlements of Trail Canyon—so named after an old miner's trail that once led up Navajo Mountain, but now was buried under a massive rock fall. That night, after a short hike and a luxurious moonlight dip, we climbed back aboard LADY JEANINE, ducked below, threw open the hatches, and fell sound asleep beneath a dome of sparkling stars.

The following morning, we continued upriver toward Big Bend country and the heart of the San Juan wilderness. After motoring east through a labyrinth of red stone canyons and mesas, we entered a large bay framed by the cliffs of Paiute Mesa. This was hard country, an immense moonscape draped in large, black boulders, gulleys, and wind-carved dunes. Except for a single houseboat that was tucked into a small canyon further south, the bay was empty, silent and unbearably hot. Not a stir, not the slightest breeze ruffled the lake's quicksilver surface. We carved relentlessly eastward, eyes glued to the depth finder that seemed stuck at 230 feet near the center of the original riverbed.

At the far end of the bay, the channel narrowed to a series of hairpin turns that carried us another five miles to the Great Bend. Suddenly, the riverbank was transformed to a glimmering palisade of amphitheaters and natural rock arches. Here, at last, was the perfect sanctuary. We made our way past one grotto and then another until we found the perfect setting: a tiny, east-facing cove with a moss carpet, wild orchids, a cluster of redbud trees, and a tiny, artesian stream. Beneath our

Jeanine peeks out from beneath the bimini. In the background a massive amphitheater with artesian springs and a natural garden

keel, the emerald waters of the San Juan River, more than 200 feet deep, glimmered opaque in the afternoon sun.

We pulled into the cove, tied off between a couple of boulders, and spent the next three days luxuriating in the warm waters, napping, listening to the brook as it dribbled into the grotto, and pausing now and then to hear the forlorn cry of the canyon wren. Toward evening, we watched Navajo Mountain turn glimmering purple in the last light or we hopped into the inflatable to explore the other grottos and coves of the neighborhood. After a brief walk ashore, a leisurely stop in a natural garden, a curious inspection of the wild animal tracks—deer, muskrat, beaver, wildcat—we returned to the inflatable and puttered back out to the main channel and on to the next arroyo or we headed back to

LADY JEANINE. I don't think we ever got over the sight of our floating home, an elegant yet modest presence in this pristine wilderness.

We read one of the local guidebooks and learned that this was sacred country to the Navajo peoples. Their stories tell how the head of Ni'go 'Asdza'a'n ("Earth Woman") is represented by Navajo Mountain and is thought to be the pollen figure or T'ad'idi'i'n Dzil of Navajoland. Traditional Navajos are reluctant to climb very high on the mountain and are fearful of the underground rumblings that have been reported on the western slopes. The Paiutes have no such reservations and have even continued to farm the northern and western canyons right up to the present.

The stones of the San Juan take their measure in time. Young rocks are 60 million years old while the venerable ones approach 300 million years. One can tell which are the older rocks, because they are delicate and easily crumble under your step. Tread carefully, be content and quiet, and listen to what the rocks have to say about this ancient and beautiful place.

Eventually, the urge to continue upriver proved irresistible so we weighed our anchors and headed farther east still, motoring slowly through the remainder of the Great Bend and past a long series of hairpin turns and vermillion palisades until we entered the expanse of Zahn Bay, the last of the large bays before the San Juan became too shallow for navigation. Here we found a tiny cove beneath the towering battlements of Monitor Butte.

That night, a cold front moved in from the north, and we were peppered by gusts that ravaged our cove. LADY JEANINE jerked at her moorings, skirting one way, and then another, while rain and waves thumped and smacked her. But her anchors remained firmly trenched, the hatches stayed tight, so it was pleasant and cozy down below. Jeanine and I played cards for matchsticks until I ran out of credit and had to wash dishes for the rest of the week. We took great care to stay clear of the chainplates, especially when the cabin turned white, illuminated by the pale flash of lightning, followed by a thunderous clap and the skies opened in a torrent of rain and hail. I lit the oil lamps so Jeanine could curl up in the starboard berth to read, while I marveled at the flash flood waterfalls that plunged into the bay, no more than half a mile away.

Desert storms can pose some unique challenges when anchoring on Lake Powell. Lightning, unexpected shallows, steep drop-offs, or fluky winds can challenge even the most experienced mariner, and tying up in small coves often requires a Mediterranean-style mooring (stern-to from a bow anchor), plus a network of lines to port and starboard.

We usually secured a couple lines to a series of large boulders fore and aft if we chose to lie beneath an amphitheater, or we set a couple of anchors at a 45-degree angle to minimize swing, especially in the lee of a point or stone outcropping. We tried to avoid beaching our sailboat, although this appears to be the preferred method for most houseboats. In any case, we always liked north- and east-facing anchorages in the lee of a cliff or battlement, because they offer shade from the intense desert sun and provide some protection from lightning and storms, which usually move in from the west or southwest. We never anchored beneath a cliff that could turn into a flash-flood waterfall, a possibility that is usually indicated by dark patina on the rocks and we never risked anchoring at the far end of any canyon where a flash flood might create a sand bar that could leave us stranded.

On the third day, we weighed anchor again and made for the confluence of the Colorado, bound for Dangling Rope

Marina, Dungeon Canyon, Page, and the Glen Canyon Dam. The dam, which is 583 feet high and was completed in 1964, just north of the Grand Canyon, created a 186-mile-long reservoir that took 17 years to fill to its planned level of 3,700 feet above sea level. Because of its many canyons and tributaries, it has nearly 2,000 miles of coastline, more than the entire U.S. West Coast from San Diego to Seattle.

The first human residents of the area, bands of prehistoric Indians, wandered the river more than 30,000 years ago. About 500 A.D., the Anasazi, which roughly translated means "the ancient ones," settled along the original riverbed and adjacent canyons, developing an advanced agrarian society that endured until about 1300 A.D., when it suddenly disappeared. Hundreds of their ruins survive today, and many, such as Defiance House in Forgotten Canyon, approximately a dozen miles north of Bullfrog Bay, are easy to visit by boat. Later, the Spaniards arrived to survey the region, and in spring of 1869, Colonel John Wesley Powell, after whom the lake is named, traversed what would later be called Glen Canyon in a small, wooden boat. In his spirit we continued south through the canyons and arroyos of the Colorado River, stopped at Dangling Rope Marina for fuel and ice cream cones. By late afternoon we found an excellent anchorage on the south shore of Dungeon Canyon. Despite its forbidding name, it is a beautiful sanctuary with steep, vermillion walls that plunge to the lake's surface, while the canyon's headwaters lead to a box canyon where an ancient sheepherder's hogan guarded the entrance to the valley floor beyond. Except for an eagle's screech and the subsequent echo, the canyon sanctuary was silent, which enhanced the spell.

The following morning, we set out for Page and the Glen Canyon Dam. As we motor-sailed past Camel Rock, a massive sandstone outcropping, the main channel opened into Padre Bay, one of the largest open-water expanses of Lake Powell. A narrows known as the Crossing of the Fathers led us through Warm Creek Bay and finally into Wahweap Bay and Wahweap Marina, the busiest stopover on the entire lake. We reprovisioned at the marina store, had a quick lunch at the beautiful Wahweap Lodge, and headed back north. As we passed Antelope Island, a forbidding black sky began to threaten us from the west and within 30 minutes, one of Powell's infamous desert storms careened down on us, in a maelstrom of whitecaps that bounced off the canyon walls from every direction. Jeanine steered the boat upwind while I doused the main and furled the headsail. Once the canvas was down, we turned north and ran at full throttle through the mounting chop, pounding up the bay at little more than two knots of speed. Spray and desert sand flew across deck, depositing a grainy soup in the corners of the cockpit sole. Seeking refuge, we ran past Castle Rock and turned due west into a small, protected cove at the far end of Warm Creek Bay. I set two bow anchors in the lee of a huge sandstone boulder and ran spring lines around some pygmy junipers on the shore. Secure at last, we tumbled below, slammed the hatch shut, and spent the rest of the afternoon nervously listening to the howling wind.

By the time the storm had subsided, it was too late to continue, so we decided to spend the night. We welcomed the morning sun with a swim, weighed anchor and headed north toward the eastern extension of Padre Bay. About three miles south of the main channel, we anchored in a tiny cove, directly beneath Dominguez Butte. To the east, the bay looked across to the crimson labyrinths of Face Canyon and the Navajo reservation beyond, while the giant stone sentinel of Camel Rock rose to the north. We went on a shore hike beneath Dominguez Butte and, upon returning to LADY JEANINE, heard the excited yelps that betrayed the presence of coyote pups whose mother no doubt just had returned from a successful hunt. We were hungry too, so we sliced up some tomatoes, barbecued hamburgers, and sat down for dinner just as a cool breeze stirred from the east. The night was clear and warm, so we slept topside in a makeshift berth while millions of stars sparkled overhead and the coyotes serenaded to the moon.

We spent three days in this cove, beneath the cliffs and sandstone arches. On the next-to-last day of this trip, we hoisted the sails in a languid southwest breeze and tacked up the bay which was tinted copper by the morning sun. It was a lovely sail, but by early afternoon the heat had become intolerable, so we motored back to our cove. For the remainder of the afternoon, we relaxed in the shade of LADY JEANINE's mainsail while the desert burned under a merciless sun. Evening darkened the azure sky as a thunderstorm cracked and boomed to the north over Navajo Mountain.

The following morning, we headed north pushed by a steady 15-knot southwest breeze. The helm was balanced, the mainsail produced welcome shade on both jibes, and LADY JEANINE picked up a bone in her teeth, as she plunged forward, running merrily through the sun's sparkling reflection on the lake's surface. We scudded 35 miles past a series of magnificent canyons and arroyos, and in the last hours of sunlight, turned at the confluence of the Escalante River where we found a small, protected cove with an artesian spring. Again we tied off between two large boulders and brought out some pillows and cushions to take advantage of an especially warm night and sleep on deck beneath the stars.

We continued upriver, stopping briefly at Three Roof

Ruin, a scattered sandstone remnant of an Anasazi settlement that had been quarried high above the river about 900 years ago. It was probably abandoned sometime around A.D. 1250 and is similar to Defiance House, which lies upriver from Bullfrog, at the far end of the navigable reaches of Forgotten Canyon. While Defiance House is notable for its flat, subterranean ceremonial chamber (or kiva) and its petroglyphs that depict fearsome warriors with shields and clubs, Three Roof Ruin is a much smaller settlement, less preserved, without petroglyphs or kiva. Nevertheless, it's worth the climb, unless one is bothered by vertigo. Jeanine pulled up to a sandstone landing so I could slip over the side and wade ashore. She then backed away to circle on the river and watch me claw my way up a set of "Moki" steps, shallow toeholds the Anasazi had chipped out of the canyon walls. The Park Service had nailed a series of cables to the cliff wall to help visitors negotiate the lower portion. Once I left the cable and steps behind, I found the climb up to the settlement steep, but not especially difficult.

Not much is left of the ruin today, except some crumbled walls, a few ceiling and wall joists, and a circular penthouse that overlooks the great wall and battlement on the other side of the river. Archeologists don't know why these outposts were abandoned. One theory is a change in precipitation patterns and recurring drought conditions during the latter part of the thirteenth century, while another one is the invasion of warrior tribes from the north. Most agree that the Anasazi, who occupied these frontier outposts and settlements through most of Glen Canyon, are the ancestors of the Hopi Indians of Arizona and New Mexico. I poked around the remnants of the tiny settlement, and tried to imagine the rich cultural and religious tradition of these remarkable people. I wondered how they might have dealt with their children in these dizzying heights (I recalled an Anasazi crutch in the museum at Bullfrog) while Jeanine was still driving the boat in circles far below. I took heart and slowly descended to the river, ever so gingerly backing down the steep corridor while a couple of large stones came loose, tumbled down the cliff and plunged into the river. Jeanine pulled up just as I jumped from the last ledge. I climbed under the pulpit stanchion and bellied aboard while she backed away and made for deeper water. She looked at me, flashed a sarcastic grin, headed up river, and muttered something about "men" under her breath. "I got some pretty good pictures, really!" I said. She just smiled and continued to steer the boat. I suppose it might have been a bit of an adventure for someone close to age sixty, but to me the reward outweighed the risk, and the pictures *were* good.

We continued on our way until the water gradually turned a muddy brown and the river became too shallow for us to go much farther. We decided to spend the night near Cow Canyon, so named for the wild cattle that once frequented the place. We made fast in the shade of an aged cottonwood among a chaotic scattering of boulders. That night, the last bronze rays of sunlight shadowed the canyon walls before we were enveloped in darkness with only the silvery specks of the stars to keep us company. One last swim before bedtime and we consigned ourselves to the company of the rising moon in a dim, blue outline on the far canyon walls.

The Escalante has been a treasure trove for archeologists, paleontologists, historians, and biologists. In 1996, a portion of the area was set aside as the Grand Staircase-Escalante National Monument and placed under the custody of the Bureau of Land Management, its first such charge. This was done to preserve the incomparable beauty of this great staircase and all the surrounding mountain ranges and buttes, and also to set aside a unique outdoor research laboratory for scientists and historians.

By the fourth day, our provisions were exhausted and we were reduced to fig bars and canned corn. It was time to head home. As we motored back to the Colorado channel and sailed north to Bullfrog, we remembered the sunsets we witnessed beneath the sandstone canopies and among hidden ruins. We also recalled the beauty of the desert sky at night and how we had been left to contemplate the mysteries of the glittering stars and the desert moon in this remarkable wilderness. For a while, the Escalante, the San Juan and the Colorado had granted us pleasure and self-indulgence in one of the most hidden alcoves on earth, as they continued on their majestic journey to the sea.

At the time, Jeanine and I did not foresee that we would soon embark on our own journey to the sea, by trailering LADY JEANINE over 1,200 miles to the Pacific to sail and explore the magnificent cruising grounds of the Northwest.

Lake Powell:
Cruising Tips for Trailer Sailors

Getting there: To reach Bullfrog, Utah, take I-70 and turn south on Utah State Route 245. Continue south on Utah SR 95 to Utah SR 276, which takes you to Bullfrog. To reach Page, Arizona, at the southern end of the lake, take I-40 and turn north on Utah SR 89. When crossing the desert, carry extra water and avoid stressing your vehicle when climbing desert mountain passes and long inclines (See Appendix, Tips for Towing). In some cases, it is advisable to turn off the AC to avoid overheating.

Launching and parking: A number of launch ramps are available at Page, and a single paved launch ramp is currently available at Bullfrog. You may park your rig a short distance from all ramps for two weeks free of charge. A launch ramp is also accessible at Halls Creek Marina, across the bay from Bullfrog, but it is a long, hard drive from any of the highways. A launch ramp was available at Hite at the northern extreme of the lake, but it is no longer in use since the water level has dropped considerably as of this writing.

Venues: The southern extreme of the lake near Glen Canyon Dam is the busiest portion of the lake and is characterized by large bays and desert fjords that are bordered by towering buttes and cliffs. The central portion of the lake is, in my opinion, the most beautiful and astonishing and serves as the gateway to the San Juan River and the Escalante-Grand Staircase National Monument. The main channel of this section winds through a series of palisades and broad channels and is bordered by majestic side canyons, secluded coves, and giant rainbow amphitheaters and natural arches including the beautiful Rainbow Bridge National Monument, one of the largest in the entire Southwest.

Since the lake depth varies by as much as 100 feet each year, no accurate charts are available, although some tourist maps may note coves and canyons of refuge and describe the layout of the canyons and natural history. In any case, as you cruise the lake, read the surface of the water for shoals (usually indicated by breaking waves and/or turquoise or muddy water). Since rock outcroppings are scattered throughout the lake, respect all channel markers and proceed slowly if you exit the main channel. Unmarked shoals or sandstone shallows may lie just below the surface— sometimes where you least expect them.

Neither the San Juan nor the Escalante have channel markers, so proceed cautiously. Avoid darkness when traveling north of Dangling Rope Marina where buoys are not lit. It is unwise to cruise or search for an anchorage after dark, since much of the lake is bordered by towering palisades, which can utterly obscure the moon.

Charts we used: We did not find any NOAA paper charts of Lake Powell, which would be constantly outdated, since the water level varies by more than 100 feet, which has a direct and profound effect on where you can launch, sail and anchor. So you need to watch your depth sounder closely, watch for muddy or light blue water or small breaking waves and ripples, which indicate shallows. Pay attention to your GPS (provided you get a signal in a steep, deep canyon) and proceed slowly when approaching an area you are not sure about, so you can back away or turn around before the water gets too thin.

We did use maps and found the following useful: Stan Jones, Lake Powell, Fish'n'Map—Lake Powell North and Lake Powell South, www.fishmap.com.

Water levels: Like on all man-made reservoirs, the water level of Lake Powell depends on the balance of in- and outflow, which in turn depend on snow pack and precipitation. This determines which launch ramps can be used and which areas on the lake are safe to cruise. The lake's water level varies widely, so check Web sites such as http://lakepowell.water-data.com/LP_WaterDB_printable.php before you go, or call the marinas to get up-to-the-minute reports about the water level and launch ramp access. Another good resource is the National Park Web site http://www.nps.gov/glca/planyourvisit/lake-powell-marinas.htm

Provisioning: You are cruising in a desert wilderness where mid-summer temperatures can exceed 110° F, and provisioning points may be separated by more than 50 miles (Dangling Rope Marina, a landlocked stopover, is the only marina between Page and Halls Creek, which are approximately 95 miles apart). Therefore, boaters should carry extensive reserves of water and fuel, especially if they are planning a side trip up the Escalante or San Juan River. Since ice will rarely last more than five days at the height of summer (See Appendix II, Sailing Well and Living Well), perishables should be kept at a minimum and should be consumed first. Stock lots of packaged and canned foods, including fruit, vegetables, canned meat, thick soups, and the like.

Fuel is available at Dangling Rope, but gasoline is extremely expensive at all marinas, so I recommend carrying extra jerry cans. However, don't carry them inside the towing vehicle as you drive to the lake, and once you have launched your boat, make sure that fuel storage is well ventilated, well secured, and shaded in the aft cockpit or lazarette of your boat.

Cell phones are of little use except in the vicinity of Page, Arizona, so monitoring the VHF radio is an absolute necessity. However, transmission and reception can be spotty and work best if you have a visual on Navajo Mountain or on the Henry Mountains in the vicinity of Bullfrog and Hall Creek Marina. A good source of information on the lake is the Web site www.waynesword.com. It provides useful information for boaters, including GPS waypoints, lake water level, launch ramps, and an area map with fishing hot spots. I found the Magellan GPS of little use, since a detailed chart of Lake Powell was not available at the time we sailed there. C-Map now offers electronic charts with the lakes of the West, including Lake Powell (C-card #NA-M020).

The National Park Service honors Golden Eagle and Golden Age Passports. Vehicle fees are $15.00 for up to 7 days, or $30.00 for the entire season; boats fees are $16.00 or $30.00 for the season; camping in developed camping areas is $8.00 per night. All boats and campers are required to have self-contained marine sanitation devices (holding tanks). Pump-out stations can be found in marinas around the lake, for example at Antelope Point, Bullfrog, Dangling Rope, and Halls Crossing.

The Bullfrog Visitor Station is open intermittently beginning in May, phone (435) 684-7400. The Wahweap District Ranger Office at the south end of the lake is open Monday through Friday throughout the year, phone (928) 608-6531. The only transportation between marinas and the backcountry is by boat, but a ferry runs from Halls Creek to Bullfrog.

Weather: As we have learned the weather on Lake Powell can change quickly and violently and that should be part of your cruising plans there. One of the biggest challenges is the short horizon, which most of the time is limited by the canyon walls around you. It is important to monitor the NOAA weather service constantly for alerts and forecasts, although the conditions may vary somewhat for your particular area. Desert storms are common on the lake, especially in early spring and during the monsoon season in late summer. They are usually preceded by darkening skies and thunderheads. Do not hesitate to seek shelter if a storm is predicted in your area.

An inflatable or other dinghy with an outboard that can be easily towed behind the boat (I recommend a double painter) enables you to go ashore or explore neighboring canyons from your moorage. They can also be useful for tying up to boulders or for setting a stern anchor.

Mooring and anchoring: Bring at least three anchors on 10 feet of chain and at least 250 feet of triple strand, ⅜" nylon line. Since most of the lake bottom is mud, a Danforth is the most effective type of anchor. A depth finder helps take the guesswork out of anchoring. However, a 20-foot anchorage may suddenly drop to 200 feet or more if you have the misfortune to set the hook beyond the edge of a submerged cliff. If you decide to spend the night in one of the numerous bays, anchor in the lee of a cliff or outcropping. If a storm is predicted, set two anchors at 45 degrees on a scope of 6:1. Anchor in the vicinity of a cliff or hill that is higher than your mast to minimize the risk of a lightning strike.

If you want to spend the night in a cove, drop anchor at the entrance and back in, again deploying enough rode for a 6:1 scope; set a stern anchor in the same manner and evaluate whether setting another hook to windward is necessary. In some cases, the stern anchor and windward anchor may be wrapped around a boulder. When anchoring in a rainbow amphitheater, wrap the bow and stern anchors around boulders and wrap the chain around the anchor flukes. Avoid the possibility of lines chafing on shore-side boulders. Leave at least 50 feet between the boat and the shoreline. Do not anchor at the far end of any canyon where you might get stranded by a shoal that can be created instantaneously by flash floods. If possible, avoid anchoring beneath a palisade where flash-flood waterfalls are likely. Check for dark patina on the canyon wall and on the rock fall at the base of the cliff. Be aware that some rainbow amphitheaters have been carved by swirling winds that also might generate powerful waterspouts.

Most houseboats prefer to put their bows on the shore and secure two stern anchors to some boulders ashore at 45 degrees. Some sailboats with retractable keels and kick-up rudders can do the same—it's called beaching—but that is a risky proposition, because a sailboat's hull shape isn't flat like a houseboat's and sand can get into the keel housing, which could jam the appendage or damage the hoisting mechanism.

Sailing the lake: The best sailing can be found north of Navajo Mountain and Navajo Ridge where cool winds from the heights flow down to the lake's surface, usually by 11 a.m. However, those winds tend to refract and follow the twists and turns of the canyon, sometimes generating a venturi effect, sometimes exploding in gusts, sometimes dying entirely. There are also some excellent sailing conditions in the vicinity of Halls Creek Bay and Bullfrog Bay where the ridge immediately west of the area generates cool breezes that flow out over the surface of the water. Such breezes may continue as far north as Cedar Canyon, north of Moki Canyon. Power boat traffic is especially dense during summer and the best time to visit the lake is in late summer, when the temperatures are somewhat cooler and the water is still quite warm for swimming. The lake is generally cool during the early spring, but the water is too cold for swimming and storms are common.

First-aid and safety: Be constantly on the alert for signs of heat stroke and dehydration, and tie up in shaded anchorages or moorings whenever possible.

When swimming, look carefully where you dive. Hidden rock outcroppings may lie just beneath the surface. As a safety rule, avoid diving from high cliffs if you are not absolutely sure that there is enough water below. Diving accidents are one of the most common causes of traumatic injury.

Wear high leather shoes when hiking, since they provide protection from snakebites, although most snakes avoid human contact. Be aware of some poisonous water snakes, even if there's only a small chance that you'll encounter them. Carry a well-stocked first-aid kit with snakebite remedies and antihistamine to treat insect bites—scorpions (which tend to lurk under rocks), black widows, and the brown recluse are indigenous throughout this region. Take careful bearings when hiking, because after a while, dramatic rock formations tend to look alike, and it is easy to get disoriented. Also, carry plenty of water to avoid dehydration. Since sandstone is very soft, be careful when climbing a rock face or walking at the edge of a cliff where the stone may crumble and give way suddenly. Never hike alone, and carry a compass, a first-aid kit, sunscreen, and extra water.

Pets cannot roam freely. Keep them on a leash no more than 6 feet long, and keep them aboard after nightfall. More than one pet owner has suffered heartbreak when the family pooch was carried off by a coyote (I personally know of a number of times when this has happened). Remember, you are operating in a desert wilderness and be aware that Glen Canyon is home to cougars, even though incidents involving humans have been rare.

Emergency evacuations from remote areas can be difficult. If you or a member of your crew have a serious accident, motor to a place where Navajo Mountain or the Henry Mountains are visible and call the park service for help with your VHF (there is almost no cell phone reception on the lake, except in the vicinity of Page). If there is no response, motor around and keep trying until you can be heard. The park service might send out a rescue vessel, so be prepared to provide an exact position, including the name and location of the canyon or channel. If it is an extreme emergency, find a flat area where it is possible to land a helicopter. I have seen a number of cases where this was the only means of evacuation.

In some cases it might be possible to hail a passing powerboat for assistance. If all else fails, head for Page, or to Bullfrog where a 24-hour infirmary is available. A word of caution: Never swim near or under the stern of houseboats when the engines are running (e.g. to charge batteries or run the AC). I know of numerous incidents of accidental death by carbon monoxide poisoning. Indeed, all rental houseboats post a warning not to swim near the exhaust.

Finally, two bits of common-sense advice: Never leave food in open areas, since it can attract coyotes and cougars, and drink alcohol in moderation since you are at more than 3,000 feet above sea level where it is easier to get intoxicated.

Part II

The Pacific Northwest

The Pacific Northwest was once our home and we remember it well: A distant sail heeled by the wind, green cedar forests and deer silently moving in the shadows. This place is defined by wind and rain—always rain—and by a bone-penetrating chill, the smell of salt air and the steady throb of ocean-bound ships, their bows slicing the water in perfect, rolling folds.

On the darkest of days, the rain clouds brood over the shorelines, the mountains hide in a veil of clouds, and the sun remains invisible, leaving only the trace of sea haze. Without the wondrous power of the sea and the eternal beauty of the mountains, this could be a horribly depressing land, held hostage all too often by gray clouds and dark forests and constant drizzle.

The other face of the Pacific Northwest is visible during the long summer days, when the sun hangs high in the sky and the sea glitters like thousand diamonds. The phrase "paradise on earth" comes to mind . . .

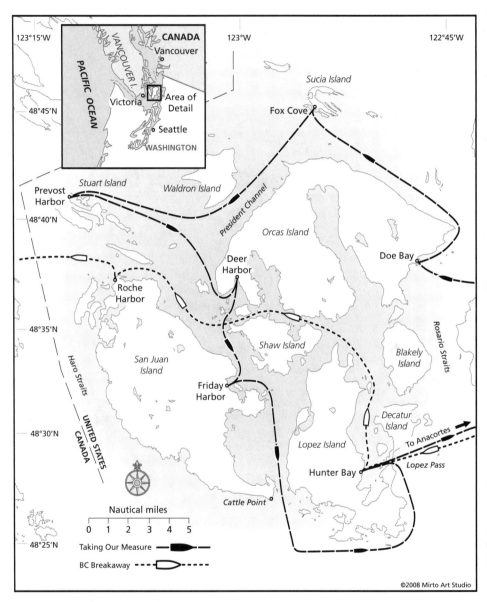

Map of San Juan Islands

Puget Sound
and the San Juan Islands

Trailer sailing, especially sailing a small boat off-shore, has always been fraught with certain risks, which include the road trip to the venue. In our case the asphalt portion of our cruise meant towing a load of 6,800 pounds across three mountain ranges as we drove from Colorado to Washington State. Even though that part of our pilgrimage to our former home on the West Coast was surprisingly uneventful, Jeanine and I felt relieved when the last pass was behind us and all that was left was blazing a path through Seattle's rush hour traffic to Shilshole Bay Marina, where we launched the boat, secured a moorage, and started our preparations for the trip north to the San Juan Islands.

Although the San Juan Islands are a favorite cruising ground for most local sailors, we knew that they could pose considerable challenges for a couple of newcomers from the high country. Therefore we spent the next few days poring over charts, tide tables, and guidebooks in preparation for our tour of the Saratoga Passage, the Rosario Straits, and the San Juan Archipelago.

We read that the currents could reach as much as six or even eight knots in some locations, while the tidal variations could be extreme, in some cases as much as 10 or 15 feet. We were advised to bring tide and current charts, detailed navigation charts for all our destinations, and to follow the daily weather reports religiously. We were also told to keep well clear of all navigational hazards. For the next four days, we took a series of shakedown cruises to familiarize ourselves with the nuances of Puget Sound west and north of Elliott Bay, but by the following week we were ready to go. We headed up the Saratoga Passage, bound for the Tulalip Indian Reservation, just north of Possession Sound. First, we enjoyed the luxury of a gentle southerly, but it gradually died and by early afternoon, the wind had clocked 180 degrees, and we were beating into a stiff northerly, doing about seven knots, which isn't bad for a 26-foot boat. As we tacked for the final beat to Tulalip, the wind slackened just a bit, but we continued to make good time and dropped anchor just as the sun was setting behind the saw-tooth horizon of the Olympic Mountains.

Tulalip Bay was a fascinating stopover since the Swinomish people have gathered here for more than 2000 years, and it has continued to serve as their economic and cultural center to this day. The bay is remarkably shallow, and we chose to anchor about three quarters of a mile from the tribal marina in 14 feet of water, about the best I could do, considering the general shallowness and the salt marsh to the south.

We spent the night visiting with Jeanine's brother, Jim, and the following morning, we made for Doe Bay on the southeast side of Orcas Island in the San Juan archipelago.

The harbor embraced a lovely tree-fringed estuary in a protected anchorage, and the charts and guidebooks were quite specific about the rustic local amenities, especially the refreshingly unconventional lodge and its non-conformist hot tubs where clothing is optional. While that sounded fine to me, Jeanine checked the guidebook and honed in on the lovely estuary with the terrific view of Mount Baker. Just like that I was overruled. I quickly forgot about it because it was time to drop anchors. I decided to trench both Danforths at a 45-degree angle, because of the considerable swell from passing container ships. After a quick, cold supper we called it a day.

The next morning we woke up to a sharp southwest. We quickly abandoned any thoughts of breakfast, weighed anchor, and bravely headed out into the Strait of Georgia. Under a full complement of sails and a gentle heel LADY JEANINE picked up a bone in her teeth as we steered a northerly course. For the next half hour, we ran downwind in heavy following seas. When we turned northwest at Lawrence Point, the gauge of our anemometer indicated an apparent wind speed between 18 and 26 knots. It was a sleigh ride.

We arrived at Sucia early that afternoon and headed straight for the Sucia Island Marine Park at Fox Cove. We managed to secure the last and in our opinion also the most picturesque mooring at the southern entrance of the inlet. While LADY JEANINE tugged at her lines and slammed a bit in the swell that rolled in from Boundary Pass, the view was absolutely splendid and well worth the suffering. That evening, a purple sunset silhouetted the flatiron of Waldron Island, while the waves out in the pass sparkled like tiny jewels. The San Juans did their best to live up to our high expectations and the lofty promise of unsurpassed beauty.

The following morning, a coy thirty-something couple

asked if we planned to stay another night. They said they had once camped here on their honeymoon, and they were without the kids for the next few days. Sucia, it seems, is an island for lovers.

Promptly but also a bit reluctantly we abandoned the coveted buoy, if only for the sake of supporting family values, and headed west with a following breeze. We hoped for a day of fine sailing, but the wind died just as we passed Waldron Island. After a brief wait and prayer or two for at least some wind, we doused the sails and motored the rest of the way through Boundary Pass to Stuart Island.

We spent the night in Prevost Harbor, a lovely sanctuary on the northwest corner of the island, and dropped anchor about three hundred yards from the park's dock. The pathways and majestic crags of the island invited us to explore. I clamped our tiny outboard to the inflatable, and we made our way ashore where we wandered beneath the canopy of massive cedars. The shadowed stillness was reminiscent of Thoreau's Walden, and we capped our walk with a swim in the sun-warmed shallows of Reid Harbor.

The following morning, we headed for Haro Strait and beat our way south and then east to Deer Harbor. A first-rate breeze was piping up from the southwest, but the tide soon got nasty. To the south, a line of container ships paraded up the straits toward Vancouver and I watched in amazement as a powerboat that looked like it was the size of a gnat raced one of these behemoths. Somehow the powerboat miraculously avoided a collision and escaped intact before it disappeared to the west.

The foul tides in President Channel were even more appalling than those we had fought in the strait earlier. Despite carrying full sail and tacking constantly, our forward progress

Jeanine at the helm. San Juan Islands, Washington

remained negligible, even as the instruments told us that we were making six knots through the water. At the rate we were going, the GPS calculated our trip time at more than seven hours, which meant that it would be nearly impossible to reach Deer Harbor before sunset. I had teased Jeanine with the prospect of a special dinner date at the old lodge, but our wretched forward progress put that prospect in peril. So I started the engine, dropped the sails, and made a beeline for Deer Harbor on the west side of Orcas Island.

This village seems lost in a romantic time warp. It has the typical feel of the San Juan Islands of old with its abandoned orchards, weathered farmhouses, rampant blackberry bushes, and untended fields. Admittedly, there were some signs of change: a new French restaurant and a complex of modern cottages, but it still retains much of the charm that I remembered when I had visited this tiny set-tlement as a child. Jeanine and I walked hand in hand to the lovely Deer Harbor Inn that was built in 1915. The food here is still served in the old crockery. Soup and salad were brought to the table and served from a common bowl; the bread steamed fresh from the oven; and the poached salmon and mussels were superb. A snobbish cat held do-minion over the place and meandered from table to table. His daily fare was leftover salmon. And our dessert came straight from the side of the road: fresh blackberries picked during the walk back down to the marina.

The following morning we sailed for Friday Harbor and on to Cattle Point further south on San Juan Island. I wasn't too sure about crossing the Strait of Juan de Fuca to Port Townsend on the Olympic Peninsula, but a sailor advised us that he had come north from Seattle under a spinnaker the previous day and saw no reason why we couldn't make it. Foolishly violating a simple rule of the sea, we relied on some-one else's judgment and accepted his recommendation and headed south to attempt the crossing.

We tacked down the San Juan Channel nicely enough and even managed to sail past Cattle Point before tide and wind came to loggerheads. However, once we were headed out into the strait, we found ourselves in the path of a horrifying westerly. When the kelp started flying, we decided that we'd seen enough, turned and ran for shelter toward Hunter Bay on the southeast end of Lopez Island.

We anchored in the bay, bore out the night, shook out the morning dew the following day, headed for Lopez Pass and Rosario Strait, and ran on a perfect beam reach eastward to Anacortes. An Erickson 32 under full sail cut sharply across our bow. Her rail was in the water and her bow wave churned

Heading up the Saratoga Passage, bound for the Swinomish Slough, gateway to Anacortes and the San Juan Islands

up a sparkling froth. Her skipper was happily wedged in a pile of cushions on the lee rail. He grinned at us, shouting, "What a great day for a sail!" I grinned back and gave him two thumbs up.

As we entered the Swinomish Channel on our way south to the Saratoga Passage, Jeanine constructed one of her hallmark fluffy, topside berths from pillows. She looked like the Queen of the Nile. She'd been an incredible help during some of the dicier moments during our pilgrimage through the islands, but now she was in her element. I offered to feed her grapes, but sensing some oblique motive of some sort on my part, she suggested that I maintain my heading and continue to steer south.

As we returned to Seattle the following day, summing up our little odyssey seemed difficult, because to me, Puget Sound and the San Juan Islands defy attempts at explanation or definition. They are all things and beyond all things: majestic, mysterious, and brooding—a seaborne country full of surprises and tiny harbors, peppered with treacherous shoals such as we encountered at Deception Pass and buffeted by winds that challenge ship, man, and mind while at the same time being dotted with strange holes and calms on the stormiest of days. I consider them a metaphor of life, forever to be explored without ever being fully understood.

As we headed back into our berth at Shilshole Bay Marina late on a Sunday evening, we watched enviously as a Cal 34 pulled out from the jetty and headed north. Perhaps, I thought, he was headed towards the San Juans, spending the night at La Conner, the next at Doe Bay, the next at Sucia, and the one after that at Stuart Island. I wished myself in his place and vowed to return, so we could also try Patos Island, the west side of San Juan Island, the Gulf Islands in Canada, and perhaps even Victoria and . . . But we'd have to do it sometime soon. After all, wasn't that why we bought the Balboa—to be free to come and to go wherever and whenever we pleased?

Foul Weather Bluff

By the first week of August, we began thinking about the preparations for our return trip to Colorado, but one more short cruise up Puget Sound was in the offing. We had promised our middle daughter, Joanna (who lived in Seattle at the time), a special 21st birthday celebration at Port Ludlow, which is west of Admiralty Inlet on the Olympic Peninsula. Although it was a major lumber port in the nineteenth century, Port Ludlow has since been converted to an upscale resort with condominiums, a golf course, swimming pool, and a 19th century hotel known for fine dining.

I was concerned about sailing north on Admiralty Inlet in a small boat, because it is the only rough-water channel in the area, notorious for its square waves. To make matters worse, the tiderips are extremely powerful, especially around Foul Weather Bluff and Point No Point, east of Port Ludlow. When the tide ebbs and the wind whistles from the north,

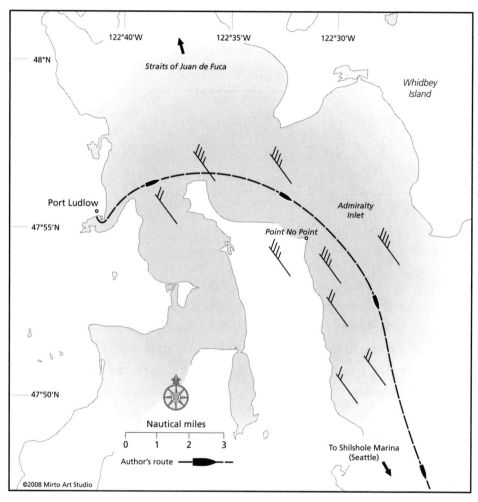

Map of Foulweather Bluff

boats bury their bows in the steep chop, which can damage rig and deck.

The weather forecast was favorable so we left Shilshole Bay Marina around noon. As we passed Meadow Point, I hoisted the main and our small genoa and we made our way north, pulled by a rather gusty southwesterly breeze. In this area, the best winds for sailing blow from the northwest, while southwest winds, though less common, usually are harbingers of low pressure and dirty weather that rolls in from the Pacific Ocean. We sailed on a broad reach, jibed right after we had passed Kingston and made for Whidbey Island, jibed again near Possession Point, the southern tip of Whidbey Island, headed west toward Foulweather Bluff, the northernmost point of the Kitsap peninsula, where we doused the sails and motored to Port Ludlow.

Despite fluky winds and confused seas it had been a decent sail. We rented a berth for the night, wandered the beach and the hotel grounds for a while, and treated Joanna to a birthday dinner and a congratulatory bottle of fine wine on the hotel veranda. But all was not well, because NOAA issued a gale warning for the Strait of Juan de Fuca, to the north of us. Soon enough the clouds thickened, and the bay was pounded by rain and lightning, which seemed to hit just about everything except us. Later we learned that the storm had spared every one in port, except a wind surfer. I have no idea why anyone would go out in such weather.

The following morning, the gale warning was downgraded to a small craft advisory, and the forecast for Admiralty Inlet suggested that the channel would settle down later in the day, so we decided to leave for the return trip to Seattle. We sailed east and south in the lee of Marrowstone Island, but as soon as we entered open water, conditions changed rapidly.

The wind increased to 25 to 30 knots apparent and the depth finder indicated a surge of about four to five feet. I double-reefed the main and furled about 40 percent of the jib, but LADY JEANINE continued to make more than seven knots on a broad reach.

Foulweather Bluff, just south of Point No Point, carries that name for a good reason. As soon as we had passed it and stuck our bow out into Admiralty Inlet, the tide ebbed north while the wind veered south and increased to 30 to 35 knots apparent. While LADY JEANINE is generally quite stable and tends to float low on her lines, we had a tough time battling a breaking chop and incredibly deep troughs. While there wasn't much possibility of broaching, our bow sometimes lurched into the air as it tried to mount the larger waves, and subsequently slammed hard into the troughs. The noise on impact was unnerving and the hobbyhorse effect simply was gut wrenching. At one point, I wondered if we might indeed crack the hull or break one of the stringers. I noticed that a couple of other boats that came down from the north had chosen to run as close to the shoreline of Whidbey Island as possible. We hugged the shore on the west side with a couple of other boats, and no one attempted to transit the inlet or to run down the middle where wind and tide were at their worst. As we continued on our southerly course, our daughter hunkered down in the salon berth where the pounding motion was minimal, but she still felt a little seasick. We finally brought her on deck to settle her stomach, but it was a miserable way of celebrating her 21st birthday. Two other boats sailed on a parallel course, immediately to starboard. Their skippers hunkered down at the helm trying to steer a straight line while their vessels lurched through the mounting seas, and I figured that we didn't look much different. Our decks were awash, the sea boiled and crested with every other wave and a gray overcast sky made the conditions look even more wretched than they were. I wondered if sunshine and a blue sea could have made this kind of sailing more bearable. But now we were trapped in dirty, northwest weather, something I had known all too well from the days of my youth when I lived in Seattle.

Years later, Jeanine and I would have lengthy discussions about the conditions south of Foulweather Bluff. Except for a storm crossing from Baja California to the Mexican mainland years later, these conditions were about as bad as we have ever experienced. I heard suddenly a terrible clanking beneath our bow. The anchor had torn loose from its bracket and was swinging, hitting and gouging the hull with every wave. I had to secure it, or we would suffer major damage, perhaps we might even get holed. Jeanine took the helm while I crawled forward, connecting and disconnecting my tether and grabbing handrails and lifelines as I edged my way to the bow.

I steadied myself against the pulpit with one hand and tried to grab the anchor with the other. I missed and almost fell over the side. I reached again, stretching precariously over the bow, grabbed again, and somehow managed to get hold of the anchor chain and pull it in. I double-wrapped the anchor to the bracket with two shock cords while the wind and spray slapped my face. After securing the ground tackle I carefully made my way back to the cockpit, sliding my safety harness along the jackline as I crawled.

I have since double-wrapped our anchors with shock cords whenever we are at sea and I have made it a habit to double-check the weather forecast most carefully when we are venturing out in unfamiliar waters. We continued south, rounded Apple Cove Point while the white caps rushed off to the east toward Point Edwards, south of the Edmonds ferry dock on the mainland. By the time we reached President Point south of Kingston, the sea had settled enough to enjoy a modicum of comfort, and the three of us were able to relax. Covering the last few miles to Shilshole Bay Marina, we agreed that we would limit our future adventures to the more benign cruising grounds of the Saratoga Passage on the east side of Whidbey Island. As far as we were concerned, Admiralty Inlet and Foulweather Bluff could be a domain for container ships, large ferries, and luxury yachts.

We were quite content to leave the waters west of Whidbey Island to adventurous souls who didn't mind howling winds, square waves, and rushing surf.

British Columbia Breakaway

We returned to Washington State the following summer, only this time we had a much more ambitious plan, an extended five-week tour of the San Juan Islands, the Gulf Islands of western Canada and the southeast coast of Vancouver Island. At the time, we simply looked forward to a grand adventure of sailing. We did not think that being cloistered aboard a 26-foot boat for more than a month was especially notable until much later when a friend wondered how we could have managed to cover almost 400 miles in such a small boat and still be on speaking terms. Only after we returned to Colorado did we realize how this experience had challenged and changed us.

Again, we launched the boat at Shilshole Bay Marina in Seattle the morning after we arrived from Colorado and spent a couple of days provisioning and studying our cruising guides, charts, and tide tables. Two days later we were ready to cast off. With the peaks of the Olympic Mountains

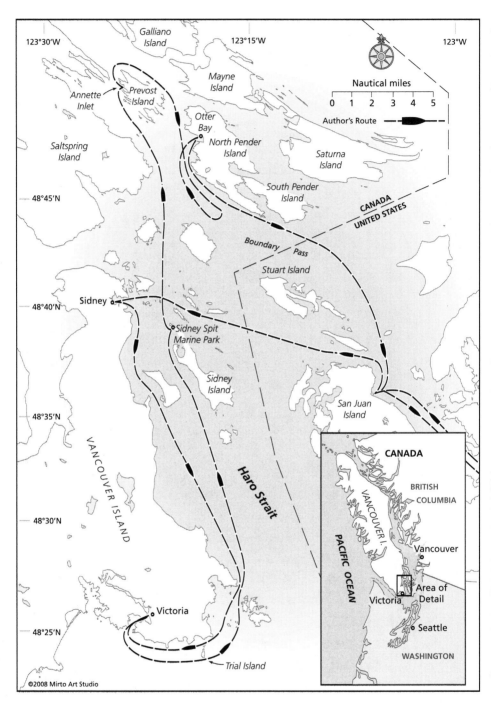

Map of British Columbia, Canada

barely visible in the morning mist, we bade the city farewell and headed north once again, bound for the Saratoga Passage, Rosario Strait, and the Strait of Juan de Fuca. Our cruising guide reminded us that the waters of the Pacific Northwest are dotted by a series of gates or passages that mark the entrance to numerous estuaries, to the north. But first, we would have to deal with Rosario Strait, which had been rather benign when we passed through the previous summer, while to the east and north of the San Juans lay the Haro Strait and Boundary Pass, gateways to the Gulf Islands and both capable of dishing out tough conditions. I felt a bit nervous, knowing that we had been lucky the previous year and would probably have to negotiate all three of these passages at some time during this cruise.

After spending the first night at Tulalip, we passed through the Swinomish Channel, the churning waters of Deception Pass and further on into Rosario Strait. It seemed that luck once again was on our side, because the strait appeared calm as far as we could see, so I rammed the throttle forward and headed west, directly for Lopez Island and Hunter Bay, where we spent a couple of days visiting my sister Kiki. I consider Hunter Bay one of the loveliest anchorages in the San Juan Islands. To the east, it offers an exquisite view of Mount Baker, a dormant volcano that stands in majestic dominion over the lesser peaks of the northern Cascades. The island is a bucolic sanctuary of madrona trees and cedars and carpets of thick mosses and wild grasses. And it's full of wildlife, too. When we explored the forest above our anchorage, a deer startled us as it bounded past and disappeared behind a cliff at the water's edge.

We stayed three nights, but on the fourth morning it was time to leave. We weighed our anchors and motored north,

Visiting the author's sister. LADY JEANINE at a mooring. Hunter Bay, Lopez Island, Washington

choosing to hoist our sails near Spencer Spit to take advantage of a fresh easterly that blew down from the Cascades. As we headed west down Harney Channel between Shaw Island and Orcas, the wires of the standing rigging sang in the freshening breeze, as LADY JEANINE cut through the building chop, leaving a merry string of bubbles in her wake. Under full canvas we sailed on a broad reach, passing lonely foghorns and tiny granite outcroppings whose steep cliffs looked like chunks of ice that were calved from a glacier. As we cut through the Wasp Passage and turned northwest into San Juan Channel, a bell buoy clanged in the distance, echoing across the waves an ancient song that was caused by the rolling sea. Was it sounding a warning, a harbinger of some sort? I hoped it would have nothing to do with us, but as we were going to find out soon enough, this hope was in vain. For the time being, though, I was content and propped my feet on the cockpit's leeward bench, poured myself a second cup of coffee, and marveled at this perfect sailing day. Little did I know what Jeanine and I would have to face within just a few days. But for now the wind shut off. We dropped the main, furled the jib, and motored the last mile to Roche Harbor on the western extreme of San Juan Island.

A charming little town, Roche Harbor attracts the fashionable and not so fashionable. We had arrived just in time for the Fourth-of-July celebration with its jumble of dock parties, barbecues and patriotic decorations. A large crowd of boaters had come up from Seattle to enjoy the festivities, and Canadians were there as well to watch the fireworks and hoist the maple-leaf flag in friendly rivalry. We found a fair anchorage at a comfortable distance from the NORDLAND, a local barge and ferry that was loaded with fireworks, which were lighting up the sky the next night with sparkling blues and reds and greens that flared into the dark as rainbows and umbrellas of fire. We stayed two extra days because of the weather, but on the third morning Haro Strait turned smooth as glass, so we weighed anchor, headed west past Henry Island, for Sidney, British Columbia. Calling in to clear customs, I couldn't help myself but ask the cheery voice at the other end of the telephone line about the expected weather and was satisfied to hear that the forecast promised calm.

On our way south, we decided to skirt the east coast of Vancouver Island, turn west at Discovery Island, and make a break for Victoria's inner harbor, all without realizing that the weather report for the Strait of Juan de Fuca now included a small-craft advisory. By the time we passed Discovery Island on the southern tip of Vancouver Island, it had been upgraded to a gale warning. Yet, we naively trusted the early reports and headed straight into this mess. By the time we passed Trial Island, approximately five miles east of Victoria Harbor, we were trapped in a narrow channel that flushed us directly into the Strait of Juan de Fuca and there was no turning back. Worse still, we were forced to take the seas on the beam, with row upon row of four- and five-foot waves tumbling over the foredeck and attacking the windward rail like snarling dogs. For an instant, we considered heading farther south to gain a better angle at the waves, but this would double the length of our journey, and the seas were building fast.

We had no other choice but to head straight for the Victoria breakwater, which resulted in an adrenaline-heavy final leg of that day's trip. By the time we reached the protected inner harbor, Jeanine and I were too exhausted to deal with the pressures of mooring in the heart of the city, so we chose to berth at the quieter government docks, west of the town's main thoroughfare.

We moored and secured LADY JEANINE and my wife, sick of being thrown around the cabin, grabbed her purse and jacket, turned her back on our little boat, and headed straight uptown to calm her nerves in the soothing atmosphere of Victoria's many china shops, which were strung out along the town's charming streets. I hoped that she would find at least a small bit of comfort in the purchase of a teacup (or two, or ten) or perhaps a full dinner set. Whatever it was going to be, it would be a meager compensation for the beating we had taken at sea.

Later that afternoon, a sharp Nordica 32 pulled into the dock next to us. Concerned that I would never get us out of this harbor alive, I hailed her skipper, a grizzled fellow with a mustache and the wisdom of the sea etched into the furrows of his brow. I explained my plight and the probability that the day's misadventure was surely going to net us plenty of new household china. Could he recommend a safe passage north to Sidney? He nodded, ushered me below to a massive nav station, and after a bit of research, consulting books and his computer (and quiet, off-key humming), he outlined a number of strategies to get us north safely, around the shoals and through the strait, assuring me that it was unlikely for Jeanine to find any excuses to go ashore for more china, *if* I followed his recommendations. Well, I'm glad to report that this fellow knew his stuff. His plan worked to perfection, as we were to find out when we left Victoria four days later.

As for Jeanine, she returned from town lugging a jumble of mysterious packages and shopping bags and her wonderful smile. With the ordeal behind us, we settled in to enjoy the charm and bustle of Victoria. I made a reservation at an old English mansion where we had spent our honeymoon 42 years before, and for a few days we traded our little boat for a room with antique furnishings and a genuine 16th century four-poster. That night, a ghost roamed the halls outside our door, and the knight in the entry moaned as he stood sentry over the brass-and-stone fireplace in the great hall. But we were just too exhausted to pay much attention, and after a while, the spooks were gone.

For the next five days, we took long afternoon naps, explored Victoria's tea shops and quaint restaurants, and visited the grand old Empress Hotel downtown. When we headed north four days later, the run past Discovery Island was a sleigh ride, just as the grizzled Nordica skipper had promised. I hoisted the sails and trimmed them for a broad reach. With the wind comfortably at our backs, Jeanine and I relaxed, munched on apples and cookies, and took in the beautiful scenery. Compared to the San Juans, the Gulf Islands have a very different geological past. While the former are essentially a sunken mountain range, the latter are made of sandstone that has been uplifted from the sea. Because of the many rocks and hazards, they are a challenge to navigate and a good set of charts is absolutely essential. Some mariners have relied on the ferries to guide them around, but this is not a good idea, because they go extremely fast and are difficult to follow.

We continued our northern course, heading for the Sidney Spit Marine Park, which is an island east of the town of Sidney. We tied up at one of the park buoys in the lee of a steep bank before we jumped into the inflatable to claim a secluded section of the beach and take a nap in the shade of an umbrella while the incoming tide gurgled at our feet. Before returning to LADY JEANINE, we went for a brief swim in the shallows of the spit in water that had closed over the hot sands and had been warmed by the afternoon sun. At dusk, a fleet of sailboats approached from the direction of Sidney, floating like feathers on the horizon as they scattered into the Gulf Islands. Later that night, the moon rose over Mount Baker and the flash of a lighthouse swept the horizon, while ferries steamed across the strait like shimmering palaces.

We stayed for three days, rolling lazily on our buoy in the afternoon swells, motoring ashore to hike the exquisite trails of the park, and exploring the salt lagoon at the far end of the spit. On the third day, we cast off, finally headed north to the Gulf Islands. As the gusts hit, they propelled us into the very heart of this archipelago, making the water under our transom churn in bubbles as we squeezed past a series of deadly shoals and rock outcroppings. I don't know whether I spent more time checking and rechecking my charts, watching for

The author at Sidney Spit, Gulf Islands, Canada

wind shifts, or simply admiring the solitary beauty of the islands. Either way, by the time we reached Prevost Island, between Mayne and Saltspring Island, I was exhausted.

We spent the next two nights at Annette Inlet, a brooding estuary of hemlock, cedar, and maple with a large saltwater marsh at the southern end. As we entered the cove, two bald eagles held dominion over the sanctuary, staring down on us from the crown of a lightning-scarred cedar, and a seal with a hypochondriacal cough surfaced and swam curiously around our boat.

The following morning, we hopped into the dinghy and motored south to the end of the bay, passing on the way countless oyster beds encrusted among the rocks and shoals like pearls in a jeweler's window. After a stroll through a lush meadow, we returned to the boat, where we lay adrift for the rest of the afternoon. "This," said Jeanine, "is a place for people who are tired of people."

On the third morning, we moved on, motoring north, along Trincomali Channel. Rounding Prevost Island, we hoisted our sails to head south on a broad reach in a freshening breeze that pushed us rapidly down the east side of North Pender Island. The sun's reflection shimmered beneath our bow, and it looked like we were in for a perfect sail to Bedwell Harbor. At this point neither we, nor the local weather channel noticed that a stalled Pacific low was finally moving inland. As we headed toward South Pender Island, the wind and chop started to build with increasing ferocity. By the time we rounded Mouat Point, we suddenly faced the mounting swells head-on. LADY JEANINE gallantly parted the crests before she dropped into the troughs, and lifted her bow high above the water to take the next wave. I cursed our luck, started the engine, doused the main, and opened the throttle all the way, but wind and tide pushed us back mercilessly. It didn't take long for us to realize that continuing east on this course was pointless. Besides, after our experience in the Strait of Juan de Fuca the previous week, neither one of us was in the mood for any more thrills.

I wanted to avoid any possibility of broaching, so I waited for the smallest possible wave and spun the helm the instant the boat perched on its crest. It was a tense moment, but LADY JEANINE responded instantly, did a lovely pirouette, and set out in the opposite direction with the boiling surf at her heels.

We made for Otter Bay on the north east shore of North Pender Island, a delightful resort with one the nicest showers we have encountered in Canada, including fresh flowers, glass partitions, and scalding hot water, all for the price of a "loonie[Canadian dollar]." As we entered the old lodge, a sun-burned, lanky gentleman who was up there in age, plinked 1950s tunes on the piano with his legs crossed, and paying little attention to the keys, while a polite audience clapped gently after each tune. We strolled down the street to a 1950s-style country store where we poked around the odd assortment of foods and curios and emerged slurping ice cream. This, we agreed, had to suffice as reward for the pounding we took during our attempt of reaching Boundary Pass, which we crossed without incident the next day. As we approached Stuart Island, we sighted three pods of Orcas, their round, black backs and dorsal fins breaking through the surface and disappearing back into the depths. One animal from the last pod stunned us when it dove under our keel and surfaced briefly on the opposite side to inspect our bow before sounding again. We checked in at customs on San Juan Island and motored east against the wind, arriving later that day close to the eastern boundary of the archipelago at Spencer Spit on the northeast side of Lopez Island, an expanse of land with a reconstructed settler's cabin, innumerable rabbits, and a view of Orcas Island and Mount Constitution to the north.

The following morning, we woke up to a slate-gray sky, which announced the arrival of another low-pressure system. But it was early, so we motored full throttle across the Rosario Strait in an effort to avoid the giant swells that would sweep north from the Strait of Juan de Fuca. As it happened, our prudence was misdirected, and we would have been better off waiting until the morning winds subsided. Little by little, the seas began to build, and I furled the jib about twenty-five percent to help steady the boat. Even so, we had to deal with a following sea that was so chaotic that it nearly tore the outboard from the transom. As we entered the lee of Fidalgo Island, the surf gradually subsided, though not without a final rogue wave or two, and it was with relief that we passed Anacortes and once again squeezed through Deception Pass into Skagit Bay and Swinomish Channel. We ran the last few miles in light rain and decided to bypass Oak Harbor so we could spend our final night in quiet seclusion in a shallow harbor at Coupeville, a sleepy little town a few miles further south on Whidbey Island.

We anchored near a tugboat, changed into dry clothing, and motored ashore to find a place that offered a dinner of fish and chips, which was easy enough. As we returned, our tugboat neighbor seemed to swing the wrong way, or perhaps it was LADY JEANINE defying tide and wind. I inquired about the puzzle, hailing, "Ahoy, aboard LORA FOSS," and three brawny figures appeared from below, among them a woman with a big smile, who looked just like Tugboat Annie. I inquired about their chain and whether I was anchored wrong or they were swung wrong, but they had no idea why they faced the wrong way and grinned and scratched their heads as they looked down on us in our tiny inflatable. In jest I offered to tow them around with the dinghy, so they would face the same direction as our boat, but they chuckled and declined and disappeared below into the warmth of the engine room while we puttered back to LADY JEANINE.

As we returned to Shilshole Bay the following day, we realized that we had conquered a magnificent venue that could challenge any mariner. We had slept in bays and harbors and we had journeyed in quest of perfect winds and exquisite sunsets and learned the nuances of one of the prettiest but also most turbulent sailing destinations we experienced. When we stepped on to dry land, another sailor warned us, "Careful, it's treacherous out there!" His assessment couldn't have been more accurate . . .

The Pacific Northwest:
Cruising Tips for Trailer Sailors

Getting there: Seattle, the Pacific Northwest's largest metro area, is fairly easy to reach, conveniently located at the intersection of I-5 and I-90. We took I-84 west to Oregon, I-82 north to Ellensburg and I-90 to Seattle. However, driving to Seattle from the Rockies as we did, requires patience and a well-prepared rig since there are several formidable passes to cross (See Appendices IV and V: "Tips for Trailering" and "Shaking down the Trailer"). For example, we had to cross four mountain ranges and eleven passes on our drive from Grand Junction, Colorado to Seattle.

Venues: We made multiple visits to this area and focused on different venues each time, starting with the San Juan Islands and expanding north past the border to Vancouver Island. Although we sought out secluded coves and anchored a lot, we were hardly more than a day's sail away from a port that offered the opportunity to provision.

NOAA Charts we used (Washington State): 18421 Strait of Juan de Fuca; 18423 San Juan Islands; 18427 Anacortes—Skagit; 18440 Admiralty Inlet; 18441 North Puget Sound; 18449 Seattle—Bremerton.

CHS Charts we used (British Columbia): 247106 Vancouver Island; 247130 Sunshine Coast; 6025803 Vancouver Island; 18433 Haro Strait.

Where to launch: The Port of Seattle operates three marinas and public docks at Bell Harbor in downtown Seattle, Elliott Bay, and Shilshole Bay. To reach Shilshole Bay Marina, our preferred launch spot, take I-5 north to Exit 166; turn west on Mercer to Elliot Ave, right on 15th, left on NW Market to Seaview and Shilshole Bay Marina, which is at 7001 Seaview Avenue NW, phone (206) 728-3006 or (800) 426-7817. Alternatively, consider launching your boat farther north in Anacortes, Bellingham, or even north of the border in Canada. Since you will be launching in salt water, you may prefer to use a hoist at one of the many boat yards that dot the coast.

Parking: You may park your rig in the Shilshole Bay Marina parking lot for two weeks free of charge and launch at the ramp that is immediately north of the marina. Another option can be found at Salmon Bay, inside the Hiram M. Chittenden Locks, a short drive towards the city along Seaview Avenue and NW 54th. This ramp is in a fresh water bay, which comes in handy for flushing your engine and rinsing your vehicle's rear wheels and brakes and the parts of your trailer that were submerged during launching.

Basic requirements: Your vessel should be big and sturdy enough to handle rough conditions with a dependable auxiliary engine that is strong enough to push the boat against strong winds and fast tide rips. A GPS receiver, VHF radio, depth sounder, a comprehensive cruising guide (see "Suggested Reading"), plus a complete set of charts with valid tide and current tables are necessary for dependable and accurate navigation.

Anchoring: Pacific Northwest tides can vary from eight to 15 feet, but many of the best anchorages are in 20 to 50 feet of water, so you should carry at least two anchors (20-pound CQR or Danforth) and about 300 feet of ½- to ⁹⁄₁₆-inch rode with 10 or 15 feet of chain. Set the anchors at an angle of 45 degrees and pay out rode with a minimum scope of 5:1. The challenge is to keep the rode short enough to minimize swinging in crowded anchorages, but long enough so it won't break out the anchor when swells are running. Make sure the bitter end is tied to the boat before you drop anchor or you'll watch it disappear like I did when I lost about $350 worth of ground tackle, because I had forgotten about the all-important hitch at the in-board end of the rode.

Weather: Although the boating season lasts from May to September, the best summer weather does not usually arrive until July. Regardless of the season, pack extra sweaters, jackets, and rain gear. Mornings are often calm so you should plan to cross open water as early as possible. On the other hand, Pacific Northwest weather can be complex and unpredictable, so include numerous ports of refuge in your itinerary. And remember: If in doubt, don't go out. Fog is a frequent occurrence, especially in the morning, so it is wise to mount a radar reflector as high as possible in the rig. This is especially important for small boats that don't have active radar and depend on others to identify their position in conditions with poor visibility.

Getting out of Seattle: When heading north from Seattle by boat, use the Saratoga Passage on the east coast of Whidbey Island. It will take you to the Swinomish Channel and Skagit Bay. You have to negotiate Deception Pass, a deep cut with fast-moving current and lots of boat traffic. It separates Whidbey and Fidalgo Islands and is spanned by a pretty bridge. On the west side of Deception Pass you enter Rosario Strait and the greater area of the San Juan Islands. This choice has two advantages. It's safe and scenic, with views of the Olympic Mountains to the west and the snow-capped Cascades to the east.

The Straits: The Strait of Juan de Fuca, Rosario Strait, and the Strait of Georgia, can be treacherous bodies of water. Trailer sailors should carefully weigh their options and double check the weather reports before attempting a crossing. Rosario Strait is especially unpredictable, flat and glassy one day and a vicious maelstrom the next, especially when wind and tide run into each other.

Crossing the border to Canada: If you are planning to cross into Canada, check your cruising guide for customs regulations, which used to be quite simple, but might be subject to change in the post-9/11 world. You will need a passport, a crew list (with passports), an itinerary, and boat documentation. When entering Canada, you will be required to check in either directly or by phone as soon as possible. Remember that only one person may leave the boat prior to checking in. When returning to the States, the procedure is similar.

For the latest information log on to Web sites such as:

www.gonorthwest.com/Visitor/planning/border/border.htm
www.cbsa-asfc.gc.ca/menu-eng.html
www.cbp.gov
www.crossingmadeeasy.com/passport-info.htm

Part III

Southern California

With each step forward, the challenges and rigors of sailing increase. The lure of new horizons brings hard lessons and sublime wonders, which leads us to a higher level of understanding and a kind of mastery we haven't known before. In other words, we are students of life, going to sea to learn lessons that can be humiliating, astonishing or plain wonderful.

Thus far we had experienced wicked desert gales on Lake Powell, and the majestic power of the Pacific Northwest. But now we kept hearing the siren call of the big water, which we gladly heeded by towing LADY JEANINE from Colorado to the coast of Southern California, where the horizon seemed to stretch into the infinite, the ocean swells sometimes looked as high as the Rockies and where we had to prove our skills in navigation, sail handling, and seamanship in a whole new setting.

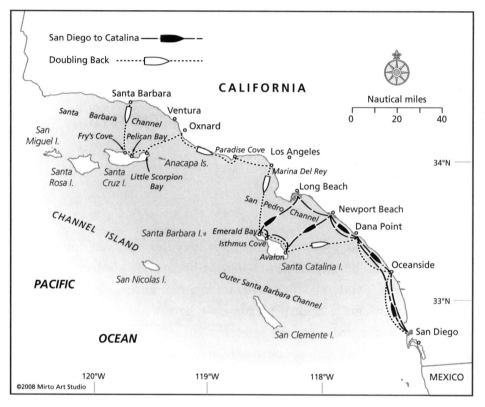

Map of Channel Islands

San Diego to Santa Catalina

The coast of Southern California is a long way from our home in Grand Junction, Colorado, and it's also a long way from the pine-shaded coves and solitary beaches that we enjoyed in the Pacific Northwest. Still, the sailing venue had a reputation of being gorgeous, with steady breezes, and opportunities to visit incomparable places. For a couple of restless wanderers like us, this was enough temptation to hitch up and check it out.

Thus, with LADY JEANINE in tow, we left the Rocky Mountains behind and traveled to San Diego for a summer's worth of ocean sailing. We managed to reserve a slip at the Bahia Resort Hotel on Mission Bay, which is a popular small-boat venue a few miles north of downtown. For the next few days, we shopped for provisions, explored San Diego Harbor, studied our charts, and played in the surf of Mission Beach.

We'd never sailed the ocean before. It's not like Puget Sound or the Canadian Gulf Islands, and it certainly doesn't mimic Lake Powell. We soon were to discover how different the game is being played on open water, which to us seemed endless, unrelenting, and somewhat intimidating. The daily weather report, although rather consistent, never failed to mention the height of the swells and the height of the wind waves. It was another one of our epiphanies of ocean sailing: Here waves are stacked upon waves.

When we finally motored out between the rock jetties of the Mission Bay Channel and hung a right to head north to Oceanside, Newport, and Santa Catalina Island, a pod of dolphins joined us and played around the boat, inspecting the anti-fouling paint on LADY JEANINE's bottom. Though we were sailing at about 6.5 knots on a broad reach, our act quickly tired them, so these playful and companionable ocean dwellers left as quickly as they had appeared.

The sailing instilled euphoria. We ran in 15-knot winds that were as steady as a surgeon's hand: no gusts, no holes, and no surprises. I was able to trim the sails perfectly. The jib was completely unfurled with a leech line as precisely adjusted as the steel guys for a high wire act. Still, the surf was a bit spooky for a couple of ocean neophytes and the swells increased with surprising speed and power as they approached land. I kept well offshore, but that didn't mean that we were in deep water. Unlike Puget Sound or Lake Powell, the Southern California coast drops off slowly. Two miles from shore, we sometimes still only had 100 feet of water under the keel. At three miles, the depth sounder still only registered a couple hundred feet.

A hurricane west of Cabo San Luca, way down on the southern tip of Baja California, had scalloped the Pacific and rearranged the prevailing northwesterlies, so we were blessed with a beam reach as we sailed north. Southern California may be packed with people, but out here on the ocean, we sighted only a few fishing charter vessels and the occasional angled feather of a sail on the distant horizon.

Later that afternoon, I heard a bustle below deck, and Jeanine emerged from the galley with a tray piled high with lunch goodies. The resident master chef had been at work, and treated me to an array of turkey sandwiches, tomatoes, cheese, crackers, grapes, melon and coffee. In my opinion a just reward for circumspect seamanship. A rewarding peck on the cheek for dessert, and she returned below to curl up in a wonderfully improvised nest of pillows and shipboard cushions. In a short while, the gentle rocking and the Pacific summer warmth lulled her to sleep. I tightened the wheel in the gentle rolls of the Pacific swells, and LADY JEANINE now only needed minimal corrections at the helm, as I watched the surf pound the beaches around Camp Pendleton.

A contingent of U.S. Marines, helicopters, and barges poked ominously out of the fog as they commenced amphibious operations. It was impressive, but I had no interest in being involved, voluntarily or otherwise. I altered course, turned hard to port to give them a wide berth. Just south of Oceanside, we crossed tracks with a gigantic blue whale. We tumbled below, threw back cushions, grabbed our life jackets and cameras, and jumped on deck again. The proximity to such a giant was marvelous and somewhat disconcerting at the same time. What if he hit us? Would we be holed? Was there a calf nearby? I changed course with a frantic spin of the wheel while Jeanine took pictures. We oohed and aaahhed and pointed and bounced around the cockpit like simpletons. The leviathan was oblivious to our presence, or so it seemed. Except for its hump and its plume and a patch of blue on its body, it was barely visible. It allowed us to take some more photographs before it turned and disappeared.

Entering Oceanside's harbor was an easy exercise, despite our apprehension about the surf and the warnings in our cruising guide. About half a mile offshore I dropped the sails, checked in with the dock master on the radio and tied up at the transient dock.

The people in this harbor are among the friendliest in California, going out of their way to help. We docked and cleaned up the boat. After all, we were from out-of-state and did not want to look tacky. Dinner was fish and chips after a short walk along the beach to Oceanside Village. The evening's entertainment was an enthralling concert by the local cats that fought sea gulls for leftovers and fishing gore.

The next morning, we headed north to Dana Point and on to Newport. We visited Balboa Island, in the center of the harbor, and found it nice, even charming with its manicured beach homes and the usual gaggle of boutiques, ice-cream parlors and fancy restaurants. Back at the dock, our neighbor, an elderly gentleman in a tired Cal 27, admitted that he didn't know where he was headed. "I jus' goes where da wind blows," he confessed and smiled weakly. His scraggy little dog cocked her head and looked up at him worshipfully. "Cute dog," we remarked. "Does she like sailing?"

"Well," he said, "I s'pose. She sure don' like to go ashore, She jus' pee where she want."

The next morning, he cranked up his diesel and hoisted sail before leaving the slip. That was a fatal mistake. As he exited the dock, the Cal promptly bounced off a sumptuous yacht that was tied up at the pump-out station. On the second pass, the old fellow managed to engrave his boat's signature along the entire starboard side of the yacht before chugging south, out of the harbor and into the Pacific. The skipper of the yacht was dismayed, but strangely positive. "I'm not going to let this ruin my day," he insisted.

From Newport, we headed across the San Pedro Channel, toward Catalina Island. As we sailed northwest, a series of drilling platforms poked out of the morning fog like giant erector sets. By 1 p.m. the winds had shifted to the northwest and started to build. Heading west, LADY JEANINE heeled to the breeze, picked up a bone in her teeth and cavorted deliciously through the swells under full canvas. At the 10-mile mark, I tacked and headed north on a close reach. When the GPS showed a 90-degree difference between our course and the bearing of the town of Avalon on Santa Catalina, we tacked again and sailed directly for the harbor. On this final leg the wind built to more than 25 knots, but I hesitated to reef, because the run was just too grand and the beauty of wind and water was impossible to resist. A short time later, after a vicious set of swells, Jeanine appeared on deck with PFD and safety harness in hand, to interrogate me on matters of sanity and safety at sea.

The last leg was a tad tougher than we'd bargained for, but we managed to reach the jetty safely. Afterwards I had to admit that my call to continue under full canvas was a little too close for comfort. But even so, we were too late to tie up inside the jetty, so we signed up for a buoy in Descanso Bay, from where we caught a water taxi into town.

We found Avalon to be a mix of Roche Harbor, Southern California chic, and Mexican warmth. Many of the shops and restaurants were three-sided affairs with cabanas and open balconies. Golf carts buzzed everywhere, a concession to the shortage of gasoline on the island. The music from the cantinas was spicy and upbeat, and the town buzzed with gentrified refugees, who had come across the channel from Los Angeles.

Santa Catalina is part of a submerged mountain range that was formed at least twenty million years ago. Later, a series of massive shifts in the earth's crust moved the island 150 miles north from the Mexican border to its present location. A fantastic ancient shoreline with sunken river valleys lies 80 feet below the surface a mile west of the island. The island's kelp beds support an extraordinary diversity of marine life, including bass, skates, rays, sharks, and garibaldi. Migrating whales, seals, sea lions, dolphins, porpoises, tuna, and marlin populate the deeper waters, and Ironbound Cove at the northwest corner of the island is said to be a breeding ground for pilot whales. There are some indications of human presence on the island as early as twelve thousand years ago. When the first Europeans arrived in the mid-sixteenth century, Catalina was populated by about 2,500 Gabrilienos or Pima Indians, who were wiped out by a measles epidemic in 1805. In the mid-1800s, the island served as a cattle ranch. The U.S. Army established a garrison there in 1863. Catalina passed through a series of individual owners and ranchers until it was bought in 1919 by William Wrigley, Jr. of chewing gum fame. Wrigley developed the town of Avalon, but the interior remained off-limits to all but a few privileged visitors. In 1975, most of the island passed to the Santa Catalina Conservancy, which has since managed the beaches, airport, and roads and has taken the lead in educating the public about the island's fragile ecosystem.

We returned to the boat later that night and listened to the music of the cantinas from the comfort of our cockpit. The next morning, we abandoned our mooring buoy and headed up the coast towards the isthmus. However, we soon were waylaid by the solitary beauty of Goat Harbor, a good fair-weather anchorage about six miles northwest of Avalon. The surf pounded against a tiny beach, and the harbor was framed by a spectacular series of rock formations. It was irresistible, and we were completely alone.

I set the anchors at a 45-degree angle, looked over the side for man-eating ocean creatures and found myself staring forty feet down into a fantasy of emerald water over a white sand bottom and tiny, darting fish. It was perfect and we spent the rest of the day swimming, beach combing, and napping in the shade of the overhanging cliffs. A gentleman in his late seventies with a physique like Batman rowed by in his dory. He stopped and we talked for a while. Then, having voiced appreciation for our anchorage, he tossed his notebook and diary into the dory and rowed off in the direction of Avalon. That night, we settled down to enjoy a lovely evening as the sky behind us turned pink in the sunset. The light at Blue Cavern Point flashed in the distance. But just as we had gotten used to this tranquility, all hell broke loose.

The evening offshore winds tumbled down a neighboring canyon and blew us out towards the channel, but the Pacific swells pinned us in the opposite direction. We were trapped! Trying to settle down, we stuffed ourselves with ginger snaps and scanned the horizon like hawks, but it didn't help much. Jeanine commented sarcastically that we should have known better than to listen to the encouragement of an elderly gentleman who had rowed more than 12 miles up and down the coast just for pleasure. Again we trusted the judgment of strangers.

We debated whether to pull out and try to reach the isthmus, but when I checked the charts I found that we would have had to pass Blue Cavern Point and round the north side of Bird Rock at Isthmus Cove in darkness, which was a scary proposition since I was not familiar with these waters. We both agreed that we were better off staying put. The moon hadn't risen, so we had little visibility, but we were in no immediate danger. Besides, the anchors were holding well, so there was very little chance for being thrown up on the beach. With that thought, we fell sound asleep. The night took on a certain rhythm: sleeping, waking, checking, sleeping, waking, and checking.

The next day, we were still alive so we weighed anchor and headed north to the isthmus, a strange and curious little village. It retains its California charm, but it has the flavor of those quaint Mexican villages half way down the Baja peninsula. The local cafe, bar, and dance hall were partially sheltered under a couple of palm trees, and the whole affair was ringed by Christmas lights and tiki-bar lanterns. Up the dusty street, the locals gravitated to a general store that sold milk, eggs, beer, and ice for top dollar.

We walked across the isthmus to the other side of the island and looked south where the Pacific Ocean rolled onward toward Mexico. The cicadas buzzed in the afternoon sun, the grass lay flattened in the searing heat, the palm trees swayed in the breezes. That night, we barbecued hamburgers and gammed with our neighbors, discussing Southern California sailing.

For many years, the isthmus has been a favorite destination for celebrities and movie stars, because it offers more privacy than Avalon. Humphrey Bogart often dropped the hook here with his beloved SANTANA. He, Charles Laughton, and Richard Burton sometimes caught lobsters (illegally) in the bay and had raucous "little-boy parties" as Lauren Bacall called them. She usually stayed behind on the mainland, which was just as well, since the boys enjoyed relieving themselves over the side without having to consider the sensibilities of female guests. The isthmus was also a favorite of Carol Lombard and Clark Gable, Errol Flynn, Lloyd Bridges, David Niven, D.W. Griffith, and Charlie Chaplin. John Wayne, too, visited the island frequently, as did Jack London aboard his famous SNARK. Robert Wagner and Natalie Wood sometimes stayed at Fourth of July Cove on the west side of the isthmus. Wood later died in a tragic drowning incident in the cove. Innumerable movies have been filmed here, perhaps the most famous of them being *Mutiny on the Bounty* (the source of the palm trees, which were brought over from the mainland) and *Rain*, starring Joan Crawford.

The next day we sailed farther north to Emerald Bay, considered by many sailors the most beautiful bay on the island. We chose to simply tie up to a buoy opposite of a rock outcropping on the edge of the inlet. We dove over the side and swam in the company of the resident bat rays. That night, we ate Jeanine's spaghetti, watched the moonrise, enjoyed the cool night breezes, and listened to the buzz of the cicadas.

We could have tarried and stayed here for the duration, but the wind called and we were voyagers at heart. We knew there were other islands, harbors and coves to be inspected. Could we blithely ignore them, simply because we thought we'd found paradise here?

Hurricane Gulch

The late afternoon winds off the San Pedro Channel usually pipe up to about 25 knots, although at times they reach 35, especially in the vicinity of the Long Beach breakwater, a.k.a. *Hurricane Gulch*. In this regard, conditions resemble those at the Golden Gate, the entrance to San Francisco Bay, especially in late summer. As the land east of Los Angeles warms with the afternoon sun, the air rises like a thermal fog and creates a low-pressure system that sucks up the cooler, denser marine air from the San Pedro Channel, resulting in a powerful sea breeze.

It had been an unusually warm summer the first year we visited California and the Mojave Desert east of Los Angeles had been hotter than usual. As a result, the afternoon breeze in the San Pedro Channel between Catalina Island and Palos Verdes in Los Angeles packed more punch than usual, especially in the afternoon, around 4 p.m. We left Avalon's inner harbor a little before 11 a.m. since I figured that we could make the 25-mile crossing with an average speed of a little more than 6 knots, which would have put us into Long Beach before 3 p.m. This meant we could pass through Hurricane Gulch before the worst of the breeze hit. The wind in the channel blew at about 10 knots when we left Avalon and hoisted sail. We were blessed with a clear sky and mild chop in the San Pedro Channel. I unfurled the light 180-percent jib, headed for the Long Beach breakwater on a broad reach and settled back for an enjoyable afternoon under sail. The GPS indicated a boat speed of ca. 5.5 knots over ground. I reckoned that later in the afternoon the apparent wind might reach 15 or 20 knots, which would have allowed us to get to Long Beach on time and in relative comfort.

By 1 p.m., we were halfway across the channel and Palos Verdes had broken through the midday fog, a sentinel that was pointing the way to Long Beach. By now, the apparent wind speed had reached nearly 20 knots, but we were making good time, and I hated to shorten sail. It was California sailing at its best. A large Beneteau passed about 200 yards to starboard without much headsail and I wondered if I should follow this example and roll up our jib as well. I gave it a try and yanked at the furling line, but we were overpowered, so it was impossible to shorten sail without heading into the wind. Since we had such a grand run, I convinced myself that we could afford to wait a little longer before reefing, so we continued to run for the breakwater at 7.5 knots over ground.

An hour later, we still were surfing along, but now at a speed that was closer to 8 knots, more than the theoretical hull speed of the Balboa 26. The measured apparent wind speed hovered between 20 and 25 knots, the keel cable was humming, and there was a good chance that the genoa might get blown out if I continued to sail the boat with so much canvas. There was no way around it: I had to bring the jib under control, so I turned into the wind until the sail started to luff, cranked it in to about 20 percent of its size, which was the best I could do since the wind pulled on the sail and wrapped it so tight that I reached the end of the furling line before the sail was rolled up all the way. I backed the sail and fell off, adjusted the sheets, and continued towards Long Beach at a more manageable speed of 6.5 knots.

But the wind was just getting started. While it continued to increase I pondered how to best douse our sails once we reached the breakwater. Usually I prefer to douse the canvas and secure the boat well outside the breakwater and enter port under engine, but this time was different. The whitecaps had built to four feet or more, and LADY JEANINE was pitching far too much to consider any action until we hit the calmer waters of the inner harbor. The way things were going I would have to make my way through the breakwater's entrance and deal with traffic while striking canvas—not a pleasant prospect. By 2:30 p.m., we were in the heart of Hurricane Gulch, with the anemometer showing 25 to 30 knots of apparent wind speed, which I considered the upper end of the range for a small and light trailerable yacht. We tore past the Los Angeles light and down the middle breakwater. As soon as we were abeam of the entry point, we turned hard to port, buried the lee rail and started the final approach to Long Beach Harbor.

Only one small problem remained: I still had to drop the main. I grabbed a handful of shock cords, took them in my teeth, clipped in my safety harness and crawled forward to drop it while Jeanine started the engine and took the helm.

She managed to head up just enough to slow the boat to about three knots, but all seemed lost because a brigantine of about 120 feet in length that had passed at our stern turned to port and pulled abreast of us to windward, while a tug and barge started to pass about 80 feet to leeward. Suddenly, we were struck by a powerful gust, which made things really interesting, because the brigantine began to fall off the wind and, with sails strapped in, heeled over on a parallel course, no more than 50 feet to port. As it closed on a collision course we were the leeward boat and had rights but, as the old adage goes, tonnage wins, regardless of the rules. So we were caught between a rock and a hard place, since we would have to deal with the tug if we fell off to avoid a collision with the brigantine.

As I contemplated all this I clambered over the cabin top to drop the main, watched by a gaggle of teens on the brigantine's lee rail, who enjoyed the action in wide-eyed amazement and waved and cheered as their vessel closed in on us. I hollered to Jeanine to keep the motor in gear and maintain as little forward momentum as possible. She also had to release all sheets of the flogging sail, which instantly cracked and whipped themselves in a tangle of half-knots and hitches. As the brigantine continued to bear down on us, we veered off to starboard toward the passing tug. I released the main halyard, the boom jogged for an instant, hit the cabin top, and the sail tumbled on top of me while the boom went over the side, dragging much of the canvas into the water.

We practically ground to a stop and started drifting to leeward, but thankfully, the tug and barge had already pulled clear. (I don't think the commercial skipper was pleased with the turn of events.) I stepped around the mast to the windward side and clawed at the wet sail to tug it back on board. Jeanine pushed the throttle forward a bit more, while I secured the sail with shock cords as best I could, tied off the main halyard, scampered back into the cockpit and secured the main sheet. Sure, the slack had piled up in an Irish pennant, but I could take care of that later when we were safe at our berth. In the meantime, I still had to deal with the jib. Now that the brigantine also had swept by without hitting us, Jeanine turned the boat into the wind until the sail luffed. Now I could let the jib out completely until it snapped and flogged for an instant, before reeling it *all* the way back in and securing the furling line and both sheets. After so much excitement we took a deep breath, turned the boat to starboard, and headed for the public dock.

That night, we congratulated ourselves on our narrow escape with a double-order of fish and chips at the Marina Village and discussed the day's mischief. Of course, the brigantine should have yielded the right of way even though she had been hit by a gust. She certainly should not have fallen off onto a collision course, which compromised our safety. If I had been at the helm of that ship, I'd have headed up to luff the sails. In any case, I remembered the basic wisdom of an old saw: "If you are thinking about shortening sail, it's probably already too late." In this case, I had set us up for a near collision behind the breakwater by not leaving Avalon sooner and by failing to furl the genoa sooner. We certainly would have had less canvas to deal with, and we would have had a good deal more control once we were inside the breakwater.

I also might have fared somewhat better if I had checked *all* the Long Beach traffic before entering the bay. This harbor is notoriously busy, and anyone entering the area should be constantly on the alert for other craft, regardless of the rules of the road—the tug as a commercial vessel had right-of-way, the brigantine did not. I simply assumed that because there were no container ships in the area and the tug was sufficiently to leeward, we would be fine. I did not anticipate the brigantine, which had approached from astern after it had swung around behind us. I also assumed that the rules of the road were understood and honored by everyone. I seem to recall a teen at the helm of the brigantine, but even so, a supervising adult should have been somewhere nearby to intervene. If such a person indeed was present, he/she was not very attentive. I have since learned that at sea Murphy's Law rules, especially if we do our part and sail with too much canvas in a place we don't know and with other, larger vessels in close proximity. In that regard, a proactive and defensive approach (another rule of the road) is most effective to avoid dangerous situations.

Santa Barbara
and the Channel Islands

We returned to California the following year in July, but this time we drove from Grand Junction to Los Angeles, took the Pacific Coast Highway north to Santa Barbara, and arrived at the marina sometime after midnight. The following morning, we secured a temporary moorage and spent the remainder of the week provisioning, resting, shopping and dawdling on State Street, and dining in the most intimate Italian restaurant I have ever known.

By the weekend, we were ready to cast off for the north side of Santa Cruz Island, the largest island of the Channel Island National Park. We had chosen Fry's Harbor as our first anchorage. It lies just in the lee of Diablo Point and once was a quarry that supplied the rock for the Santa Barbara breakwater. Today, only a collapsed derrick and some remnants of railway track survive. As we entered this lovely cove, we were surrounded by cliffs while the quarry framed the entrance to a large canyon that cascaded down from the upper reaches of

Preparing to launch. Santa Barbara, California

the island. Our guidebook suggested that we anchor as far to the west as possible, and I set double hooks fore and aft to remain in the "dead zone" which is a sweet spot between the dying wind that came off Diablo Point on our starboard side and the canyon breeze that expired a couple of boat lengths to port.

We took the dinghy ashore for a quick swim, and a hike up the canyon before returning to LADY JEANINE to prepare our first dinner on board—New York steaks, fresh tomatoes, fresh peaches—all enjoyed beneath the golden glow of our little brass oil lamp. An evening in this setting was perfect for romance, and we opened the hatch to sleep beneath the stars while a velvet breeze swirled through our cabin.

With 96 square miles, Santa Cruz Island is the largest one of the eight islands in the Channel Islands National Park. It is

At anchor, Santa Cruz Island

called the Galapagos of North America because it supports more than 1,000 different species of plant and animal wildlife, and it is one of the finest cruising destinations on the West Coast with every kind of scenery imaginable: steep cliffs that fall straight into the ocean, low, grassy hills, dunes and sandy beaches and secluded, rocky coves. The first inhabitants, the Island Chumash, settled here in a dozen villages and numbered over 2,000. Like the Pima Indians on Catalina, the Chumash suffered terribly from a measles epidemic in the early nineteenth century, which nearly wiped them out. The remainder was forced to leave and resettle on the mainland. For a long time, the island was under various private owners who used it for livestock farming. But now, the western three quarters are owned and managed by the Nature Conservancy, which requires permits for access, while the eastern quarter is

Departing Santa Barbara and heading south for Fry's Harbor, Santa Cruz Island

owned and managed by the National Park Service, which doesn't require permits for visitors who come by boat.

Get used to the fact that there are no buoys or formal anchorages anywhere along the island's 77 miles of craggy and dramatic coastline. (See sidebar for more information.) We stayed at Fry's Harbor for two days before heading a few miles east to Pelican Bay, another lovely spot to drop the hook. Pelican is surrounded on all sides by fantastic cliffs that are draped with a patchwork of wild flowers and hanging vegetation. In the hills and canyons above, oak trees and evergreens and some remnants of an old lodge that flourished here in the 1920s remind visitors of the island's busy past.

Jeanine and I motored ashore to a worn stairway that

had once led to the resort. Not much of the place is left, only some concrete pylons, a stone pathway, and a retaining wall that seemed to crumble before our eyes. We walked to the point that looked out over the water as the afternoon winds began to wreak havoc in the Santa Barbara Channel. The mainland was barely visible, while far to the west a container ship emerged from the fog as it headed for the Port of Long Beach. We stayed at Pelican another two days before we set sail for Little Scorpion Anchorage, a cliff-fringed bay on the island's eastern tip that is rather exposed to the elements. For that reason I edged as far back from the channel as possible and set double anchors in the lee of a massive rock overhang.

Later that evening, a powerful easterly ruffled the surface of the bay, and I wondered with a pang of panic if this might be the onset of the infamous offshore breeze, the Santa Ana, although this was the wrong time of year. I dropped into the inflatable, motored over to a small lobster boat, and hailed the skipper. A large hulk of a man with tousled hair and a St. Christopher medal around his neck emerged from the cabin and peered down at me.

"Is that the beginning of a Santa Ana?" I asked.

He looked eastward and ran his fingers through his hair. In a kind voice but in broken English, he assured me that the wind would die in an hour or so. Nothing to worry about. He clung to the gunnels to keep his balance and looked over at our sailboat as it bobbed up and down like a duck in a hurricane.

"It'll be okay," he said and went below.

Sure enough, the winds died in less than an hour, and LADY JEANINE settled in for a quiet night. Two hours later, I checked on the little lobster boat, but it was gone. It had disappeared into the night and left us behind, alone beneath the stars.

The following morning, we left for the mainland. As we headed north, the wind began to fill in from the northwest. By the time we reached mid-channel it clocked in at 20 knots with gusts of 25. The channel started to look like a potato patch. Our trusty little boat parted the crests and surfed down into the troughs until the keel cable buzzed and the hull began to rumble. It was a lively reach across, even under reefed main and fifty-percent jib. At one point, after a series of particularly nasty swells and bumps, I peeked below to see how the first mate was faring. All I could see were her toes, which were not yet curled, so I figured she must be okay. I later found out that she had cursed the gods of the wind and the sea and resigned herself to endure a miserable afternoon of surf and salt spray. She had then buried herself in a copy of *The Perfect Storm* and comforted herself in the knowledge that this, like the momentary gusts at Little Scorpion, was probably nothing and would probably come to nothing.

We spent the night at Anacapa Marina in Oxnard, relaxed at the pool, reprovisioned at the nearby shopping center, and headed down the coast two days later, aiming for Paradise Cove near Santa Monica. As we rounded Point Dume, I looked for the cove, but could find nothing although I had copied the GPS coordinates from our cruising guide. Finally, in exasperation, Jeanine checked the charts. Her serious look turned to a mischievous grin as she pointed to the words "Paradise Cove" imprinted across a relatively broad area, just east of the point. This had to be the "anchorage," even though surf crashed against the beach. I hesitated to drop the hook in such an exposed location and decided to row ashore to take another bearing of this popular anchorage and appraise our prospects for surviving the night.

It's no secret that the best-laid plans sometimes go awry and this was my time to get reminded of this simple truth. Just as I approached the beach, I looked up and noticed that I had drifted into the surf zone and that I was in the path of an approaching breaker. As the monster bore down on me, it looked like a Tyrannosaurus Rex at full height. I cursed under my breath as I helplessly watched the wall of water above my head and braced for the impact. The next instant, I was tossed headlong overboard and got buried by the wave, while the inflatable tumbled ashore. Coffee cup, shoes, oars, sweater, and the boat washed up on the beach, scattered every which way on the sand. The scene resembled a junkyard sale. At the time I had no way of knowing, but later I learned that my wife had witnessed the entire drama in horror from afar.

An Italian wedding party came to my rescue. Grandma wanted to take me home and dry my clothes. The groom and the best man wanted to perk me up with *vino*. The bridesmaids wanted to feed me cheese and sandwiches.

"Is this Paradise Cove?" I asked, looking rather forlorn and drippy.

"Yes, yes," came the reply.

"Is my boat anchored properly?" I wanted to know.

"Yes, but are *you* okay?" they asked.

"Yes, I'm fine! Thank you!" I replied.

I gathered my belongings, minus my favorite coffee cup that had gone awol and plotted my exit. Mortified, I tried to time the breakers, launched the inflatable on the crest of a smaller wave, scrambled aboard, and paddled quickly back to the boat to reassure Jeanine that I had survived the caper only a little worse for wear. Early the following morning, she woke me concerned about the surf that was breaking dangerously close to our boat as the tide receded. In less than 10 minutes we pulled out, just in time to avoid being tossed ashore. When we realized how serious it was, we scrambled on deck without bothering to dress, pulled up both anchors, started the engine, and motored out into the fog and deeper water. When we finally could barely hear the surf, I took a deep breath, turned off the motor and went below to dress and brew a pot of coffee. Later we talked about the morning's escapade and resolved to avoid anchoring in less than 40 feet of water when we were backed up against a California beach, regardless of popular opinion or the advice in the cruising guide. Later that morning, we puttered past Malibu, picked up a breeze near Santa Monica and sailed down to Marina Del Rey, still one of the largest man-made yacht harbors in the world, to spend the night at the public dock.

The following morning found us reaching across the San Pedro Channel. LADY JEANINE was heeled over enough to put her lee rail under water, and her bow sliced through the chop while the afternoon sun turned the flying spray into jewels. Soon, a pod of dolphins emerged alongside to play. Some of them crossed under our keel and popped up on the opposite side while others jumped and twisted in the crest of our bow wave and in our wake. It was hard not to get caught up in the moment, communing with these intelligent beings who live in another element, so Jeanine and I jumped around the cockpit excitedly, trying to get the best view of the show.

Soon the dolphins disappeared, leaving us alone on our way to Santa Catalina Island. When we arrived at Emerald

Bay, there was enough time left to swim in the crystal-clear waters and lounge on the tiny beach of the cove, before sitting down for a dinner of sinfully delicious seafood, and watching the moon light up the interior of our cabin. We stayed to enjoy this idyll for two days before we weighed anchor and sailed east to Two Harbors where we anchored near the northern end of the bay. Just as we settled in, a classic ketch pulled up next to us, skippered by a salty looking individual with straw hat and overall, who had help from a swarthy, muscular woman, who could have been of Polynesian descent with her shiny, long black hair.

They anchored in the same puzzling manner that I had seen quite often in California: the skipper tossed the hook over the side and watched it disappear into the deep. After a few moments and without so much as a word or gesture, he went below leaving it to fate and chance for the tackle to fetch up or to slip away, which would have set his ship adrift toward the open ocean.

On the next morning he was gone. Whether he weighed anchor in style or simply drifted away with his hook still hanging over the side, I shall never know. The following morning, we sailed east along the island's coast to Avalon. Again, the harbor was choked with a huge variety of watercraft. We took the dinghy ashore for a terrific Mexican dinner in a cantina, looked around shops and boutiques on Crescent Avenue, and returned to LADY JEANINE as the evening faded away and the lights of Avalon went out one by one.

Next on our itinerary was Dana Point, the town named after Richard Henry Dana Jr. who wrote *Two Years Before the Mast*. Getting there we had a good laugh watching the antics of junior sailors who cut their teeth on small dinghies, fumbling, bumbling and heeling precariously while fouling their lines with absolutely no fear of the consequences. A chase boat with concerned adults monitored the munchkins, trying to save them from capsizing or from being carried out to sea.

Later that evening, a tired old ketch with a young couple pulled in next to us. The woman had a tan and was cradling a small baby, while her male companion, a strapping young man with sun-bleached hair, looked like he could have been at home on a surf board (of which they carried two). They might have come in from south of the border and my suspicion about their vagabond life was confirmed when both vessels had swung around far enough so I could read the boat's name, FREEDOM. To me that was a wonderful declaration and something in me envied them for the courage of this statement. Some day, Jeanine and I might follow in their wake to live free and to come and go with the wind.

As we pulled into San Diego, I realized that our addiction to sailing would never be satisfied, that Jeanine and I would never want to forget the brilliant days, fragrant evenings and the sound of the wind rustling the trees. Perhaps that was the essence of sailing: A patchwork of colors, a canopy of stars, wind, waves and unforgettable experiences that come with the freedom of chasing the horizon under sail.

We vowed to return soon.

The Southern California Coast: Cruising Tips for Trailer Sailors

Getting there: Driving to Southern California from Colorado, as we did, can be done along different routes. The most obvious is taking I-70 west to Utah and I-15 South to Los Angeles or San Diego. The other option is taking I-25 south from Denver to Albuquerque, NM, then I-40 west, across Arizona to Barstow, California, just east of Los Angeles, where it intersects with I-15. Either way you'd have to cross passes in the Rockies, some of them as high as 10,000 feet above sea level, and you have to deal with the notorious Mojave Desert. If you drive during summer, you should consider crossing it at night, since daytime temperatures can and will exceed 110° F.

Before getting on the road for this trip it is especially important to inspect tires, brakes and the cooling system of your vehicle since they will have to endure some taxing conditions. Your vehicle needs to be strong enough to climb those passes and the AC might have to be switched off to avoid overheating, especially when driving long, steep hills south of Vegas in mid-summer. Don't stress your towing vehicle by driving too fast, carry extra water, and consider turning off the air conditioner during long ascents. Use engine brakes during lengthy descents to avoid brake fade or overheating.

Finding moorage and launch ramp: Transient moorings and anchorages are available in almost every city from Santa Barbara to San Diego. Log on to www.sailorschoice.com/Harbors.htm to find out more about marinas and launch ramps along the Southern California coast.

If you plan to cruise the coast of Southern California during the summer months and don't want to run into the northwesterlies, set it up as a one-way trip and launch your boat at the northernmost point of your route. This allows you to sail downwind or on a reach with the prevailing winds. It's different in the winter, with a high likelihood of offshore breezes (the infamously hot and dry Santa Ana winds) or strong southwesterlies, which herald bad weather and should be avoided altogether, because they can produce dangerous seas when they run into swells from a different weather system farther north.

At many marinas you have the option for hoist-launching your boat, thus saving vehicle and trailer from salt-water immersion. If you elect to use a launch ramp, take the vehicle and trailer to a freshwater hose or a car wash as soon as possible and rinse them thoroughly (axles and brakes).

Parking: Parking is possible at public ramps, from five days to two weeks, sometimes even more. But, sad to say, deserting your vehicle and trailer for a long period increases the risk of theft and vandalism. If you want to play it safe, especially if you are planning an extended voyage, consider parking your rig in a secure lot that is well lit at night and possibly guarded. It's a little bit of a hassle, since there are often restrictions on vehicles with trailers, but for peace of mind it might be worth it. Carefully read and follow all rules and regulations in public parking facilities to avoid being towed and impounded.

Venues: In my opinion, the best venues for extended cruising the California coast on a trailerable sailboat are the areas south of Santa Barbara, simply because the water and air temperatures are warmer than in Northern California, which has a profound effect on the gear you need and the kind of sailing you'll be able to enjoy. Except for San Francisco Bay and the San Joaquin River Delta, Central and Northern California don't offer protected venues for small-boat cruising. Wherever you go, you will have to sail the open ocean and you will have to prepare to handle some rough conditions since suitable ports of refuge such as Santa Cruz, Monterey or Morro Bay are few and far between.

NOAA Charts we used: 18720 Pt. Dume to Purisma, 18728, 18729 Santa Cruz Island; 18740 Santa Rosa Island; 18746 San Pedro Channel; 18757 Catalina Island; 18773 San Diego Bay; 18774 Gulf of Catalina.

Channel Islands National Park: This is easily one of the most fascinating and beautiful cruising venues on the West Coast. Breathtaking scenery, variety and abundance of wildlife, secluded and safe anchorages and some incredible sailing can be found in this area, which lies approximately 25 miles offshore. There are numerous options to access the Channel Islands from Santa Barbara, Ventura, and the aptly named Channel Islands Harbor in Oxnard. The Park Service does not charge for access of the five islands (Anacapa, Santa Cruz, Santa Rosa, San Miguel, and Santa Barbara), but will take a $15.00 fee for campsite reservations. The park is open all year but the visitor centers in Ventura and Santa Barbara are closed Thanksgiving and December 25.

A landing permit is required for the western portion of Santa Cruz Island that is owned and managed by The Nature Conservancy (TNC). Contact scilandingpermit@tnc.org or log on to http://nature.org/ for a permit and allow at least 15 business days for processing. There are no mooring buoys or marinas anywhere on the islands, so you will need to bring solid ground tackle and plenty of rode to moor your vessel safely in any one of the park's wild anchorages.

The islands of Santa Rosa and San Miguel farther to the west should only be attempted if you have considerable experience in heavy weather sailing. Anacapa, which is the easternmost of these islands should be visited only during the day; the western part of the island is off-limits to visitors because of the brown pelican rookeries.

Weather conditions in the Santa Barbara Channel and around the islands are variable. Only experienced boaters with sturdy vessels that are capable of withstanding severe weather should make the cross-channel passage. Always get the latest weather broadcast from the NOAA Weather Service (805) 988-6610, or by visiting the Channel Islands National Marine Sanctuary's Internet Weather Kiosk http://channelislands.noaa.gov/, and under way by monitoring the radio on VHF-FM 162.475 MHz (Weather Channel

3) for marine forecasts and VHF-FM 162.55 MHz (Weather Channel 1) and VHF-FM 162.40 MHz (Weather Channel 2) for land-based observations.

Sailing conditions vary considerably in the channel. The calmest time generally is from August to October. Count on high wind and seas with sudden changes during the remainder of the year. Forty-knot winds are not unusual for Santa Rosa and San Miguel Islands, while conditions around Anacapa and Santa Barbara Islands are more moderate. It's often calm in the early morning and breezy in the afternoon. Prevailing wind direction is northwest, but from September through April you should be prepared to encounter periods with strong easterly Santa Ana winds.

Dense fog, like almost everywhere along the California coast, is common during the summer months, so exact navigation is more than a virtue. Ocean currents of considerable strength may be encountered both near and offshore from the islands. Ocean water temperatures range from the lower 50°F in the winter to the upper 60°F in the fall.

For more information, visit:

http://www.nps.gov/chis/planyourvisit/boating.htm

http://channelislands.noaa.gov/

http://www.nature.org/wherewework/northamerica/states/california/preserves/art6335.html

Basic requirements: As for cruising the Pacific Northwest, you'll need a stout little vessel with a strong enough auxiliary engine that can handle rough water and high winds, especially if you are planning to cross the San Pedro or Santa Barbara Channel.

Since you will be sailing big swells in a small boat, wear a safety harness, tether, and PFD at all times. Remain in the cockpit unless it is absolutely necessary to make your way forward to hoist or drop your sails or set an anchor. If you haven't done so already, consider re-rigging your boat so you can operate all halyards, sail controls and reef lines from the cockpit.

Storms and ports of refuge: Unlike central and northern California, the coast south of Santa Barbara offers more suitable ports of refuge. Keep a weather eye and monitor the NOAA weather channels at all times, but keep in mind that this is a big area and the weather reports tend to generalize. In other words, conditions in your particular location may vary. You may also monitor raw data from numerous coastal, offshore weather buoys www.nws.noaa. gov/os/marine/marine_map.htm. Click on the nearest cities (e.g. Los Angeles or San Diego) to get the detailed map with the weather buoys. Then click on any of the buoys to get the current forecast.

Fog is a constant as we've mentioned already. Don't complain, but deal with it. Hoist a radar reflector and be flexible in your trip planning. If the soup is too thick, stay put and wait until the sun becomes strong enough to burn it off, mostly around late morning or noon. On the other hand, afternoon breezes can be quite brisk, especially in the San Pedro and Santa Barbara Channels so simple and effective reefing systems like a roller-furling jib and a single-line reef for the main are a big safety factor, because you don't have to leave the cockpit.

In any case, if the National Weather Service issues a *Small Craft Advisory* (wind speed between 21-33 knots) they mean people like you, because a trailerable boat is a small craft. If you ever found yourself battling conditions that qualified for a small-craft advisory, you know that the weather folks use this term for good reasons.

Sailing advice for this area wouldn't be complete without a word about Point Conception, which is known as the Cape Horn of the Pacific. Most of the California coast runs more or less north to south but not along the Santa Barbara channel. There the land runs nearly east to west and at the west end of the channel, it abruptly turns 90° degrees northward, which makes it the most exposed point along this coast and extremely challenging to navigate, even on calm days. Juan Rodríguez Cabrillo tried it first in 1542 and was thwarted. He fled to San Miguel Island, where he died. His second-in-command didn't fare much better. Sixty years later another Spaniard, Sebastián Vizcaíno, came along, and named this vicious little cape *Punta de la Limpia Concepcion*. Try it if you must, but only show up if you're ready for battle.

Anchoring: Carry at least two anchors of 18 to 25 pounds. Unless your little yacht has an electric windlass, that's enough weight to haul up manually, especially when you have 200 feet or more of rode in the water. The best style of anchors are either a plow, a CQR, or a Danforth on 10 to 15 feet of chain and approximately 250 feet of $\frac{3}{8}$" triple strand nylon rode. Anchoring bow and stern (similar to mooring Mediterranean style) is often a necessity at Santa Catalina Island and Santa Cruz Island where an evening breeze can whistle down the canyons and might swing a conventionally anchored boat broadside into the prevailing winds and tides. If you think that taking waves on the beam is uncomfortable while sailing, try it while anchored. It's pure misery.

Contacts: The Harbor Patrol office in Santa Barbara is located on the second floor of the chandlery and monitors VHF Channel 12 & 16. For Harbor Patrol assistance call (805) 564-5530. If the harbor is full, anchor east of Stearns Wharf, except in southeasterly winds.

The Ventura Harbor Master's office is on the point north of the entrance basin and monitors VHF Channel 16, the telephone number is (805) 642-8618. Don't attempt to enter this harbor at night or in high swells or heavy westerlies, because of the shoaling north of the entrance.

The Channel Islands Harbormaster can be reached 24 hours a day on Channel 16. The office is located on the east side of the harbor. The office monitors VHF Channels 12 or 16 or during business hours it can be reached by phone at (805) 382-3007. Call for your berth assignment at one of the numerous marinas. This is a lovely harbor, well maintained with excellent facilities.

Marina Del Rey Harbor Patrol, (310) 823-7762 or VHF

Channel 12. With more than 10,000 berths, this is still one of the largest man-made yacht harbors in the world. It has excellent facilities, and guest slips are available at both private marinas and county-owned Burton Chase Park. Vessels under sail should use the center lane in the harbor entrance but I strongly recommend to motor in on your first visit.

Los Angeles/ Long Beach: You can enter via Long Beach and the gap in the main breakwater. Moorings are available throughout the harbor, including Long Beach Harbor, Rainbow Marina and Alamitos Bay. This is one of the busiest commercial ports in the world, so be alert, watch for traffic and steer clear of all commercial vessels. To get a guest slip, contact the individual marinas or hail the harbor masters on Channel 16.

Long Beach Shoreline (Downtown) (562) 570-4950; arrangements for guest slips may be made at the office on the end of the point at the entrance to the marina or by phone. Reservations are secured by check and are recommended for holidays and weekends.

Rainbow Marina (562) 570-8636; www.longbeach.gov/park/marine/rainbow.asp. Alamitos Bay Marina (562) 570-3215; www.longbeach.gov/park/marine/alamitos_bay.asp

Catalina Island: Catalina Island is a perennial favorite of California sailors, pretty, scenic and crowded, especially during the season and on weekends. Prepare to accept alternatives if you can't find a mooring in the packed harbor. Catalina Harbor is Santa Catalina Island's most protected harbor. There are 97 moorings and an anchorage for more than 200 boats. There is a dinghy dock, pump-out services, and on-shore picnic facilities. From the dock, it's a half-mile walk on flat terrain to the village of Two Harbors. A shuttle is available on summer weekends. The Catalina Harbor Department at Two Harbors can be reached via VHF Channel 9 or by calling (310) 510-2683x2.

Avalon is crowded and the authorities are keeping an eye out for boaters who discharge their holding tanks illegally. The Avalon Harbormaster can be hailed on Channel 12 or 16 or reached by phone (310) 510-0535 or VHF Channel 12. If you need to have your head pumped out, call VHF Channel 68 or (310) 510-3215.

Newport Beach: For guest slip and temporary anchorage information, boaters should call the Harbor Patrol office in Newport Beach on VHF Channel 16 or at (949) 723-1002. The Orange County Harbor Patrol is at (949) 723-1000. Anchor east of Lido Island in this enormous harbor with numerous private docks, moorings, restaurants, and shops. Guest moorings are available through the harbormaster for a nominal fee.

Dana Point: A marina company manages the guest slips for the harbor for vessels up to 65 feet. Call (949) 496-6137 for reservations, slip assignment and fees. For emergencies, hail the Harbor Patrol on VHF Channel 16, for normal business call them at (949) 248-2222.

Oceanside: The entrance to this harbor is tricky, especially in strong southeasterly winds. Even though there is no anchorage in the harbor we rank Oceanside as one of the most congenial ports on this coast. The Harbor Police operates 24 hours. Their building is slightly to port, past the motel. You can tie up at the guest slips and walk to the office to get your berth assignment. They monitor VHF Channel 16 and talk on 12 or you can reach them via telephone at (760) 435-4000.

Mission Bay, San Diego: The Mission Bay Harbor Patrol offers assistance 24 hours a day via VHF Channel 16. For guest slips call (619) 686-6227. The office is open weekdays from 8 a.m. to 5 p.m. Slips and a few protected 72-hour moorings are available at the north end of Mariners Basin, call (619) 221-8800. You may stay up to three days out of a seven-day period at no cost. If you prefer to stay closer to downtown in San Diego Bay, you have to continue about 5 miles south and round Point Loma.

San Diego: Harbor Police (Transient Boat Dock at Shelter Island) can be reached via VHF Channel 16 or by phone (619) 686-6227. To inquire about moorings, call (619) 291-0916. Other helpful numbers are Emergency Dispatch (619) 223-1133; non-emergency (619) 686-6272.

The mooring office and dock are located on the southern end of Shelter Island, at the entrance to the Shelter Island Yacht Basin. Although reservations are not accepted, you may contact the Shelter Island Mooring Office to inquire about the availability of slips. Docking/mooring facilities in San Diego Bay can be found at Harbor Island, Coronado, Glorietta Bay, South San Diego Bay, and Chula Vista. This is a Navy town, so keep away from warships, which are berthed throughout the bay.

Part IV

Mexico

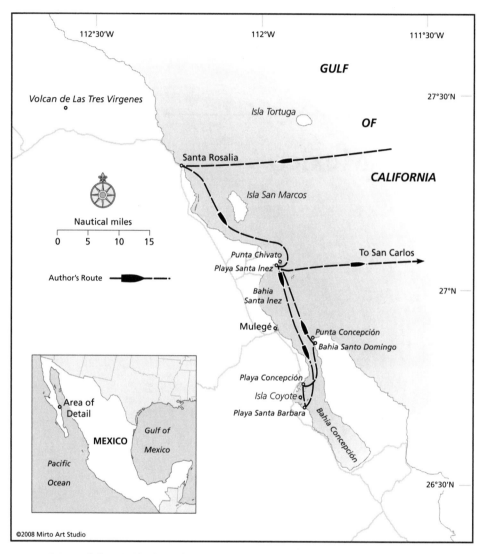

112°30′W   112°W   111°30′W

GULF

Volcan de Las Tres Virgenes

27°30′N

Isla Tortuga

OF

Santa Rosalia

CALIFORNIA

Isla San Marcos

Nautical miles

0   5   10   15

Punta Chivato

To San Carlos

Playa Santa Inez

Author's Route

27°N

Bahia
Santa Inez

Mulegé

Punta Concepción

Bahia Santo Domingo

Playa Concepción

Area of
Detail

Isla Coyote

Gulf of

MEXICO

Playa Santa Barbara

Bahia Concepción

Mexico

Pacific

Ocean

26°30′N

©2008 Mirto Art Studio

Map of the Gulf of California

A Baja Sojourn

During the early spring of 2002, Jeanine and I took an extended trailer-boat cruise on the Gulf of California. Our temporary homeport, Marina Seca in San Carlos, was 230 miles from Nogales on the U.S. border and a little less than a thousand miles from our home in Grand Junction, Colorado. Although it was an ordeal towing a trailer boat that far, we were sufficiently prepared and hoped that the ordeal of getting there would be richly rewarded with some fantastic cruising in this venue. The Gulf of California, as it turned out, lived up to our highest expectations. The mainland's coast along the Gulf's Midriff area offered more than 40 separate anchorages within 60 miles of San Carlos, and the Baja peninsula, 90 miles to the west, is the last great desert wilderness in North America. All we needed was a break in the weather for the crossing.

Highway 15 from the town of Nogales to San Carlos is a narrow four-lane toll road with almost no shoulders that meanders through the town of Hermosillo and a number of small villages along the way. We tried to avoid night driving, although we knew of some boaters who preferred the convenience of less traffic and cooler temperatures. But to us, the potential dangers outweighed the advantages, e.g. sharp and unexpected curves, and livestock wandering into the narrow lanes.

Crossing the border to Mexico is much easier today than it used to be when we visited. Nowadays, it's only necessary to check in once, show your passport, submit a temporary import permit for both car and boat, and provide proof of insurance. At the time we visited, border and port authorities demanded special fees, proper stamps, proof of insurance, and the vessel registration. We also had to present our documents at every street corner: to the marina, to immigration, to the port captain, and the port authority. Sometimes this procedure could take as much as half a day.

The northern Gulf of California is an area of extreme temperatures, salinity, and tidal differences that can reach 20 feet or more. There wasn't much we could do about tides and temperature, but at least we kept truck and trailer away from the salty brine. We paid for a hoist to launch our boat. Even with the 10-peso tip for the workers it was a minor expense that helped minimize corrosion on the vehicle and the trailer. We had chosen San Carlos as our temporary home base for very specific reasons: It was outside the hurricane alley that runs farther south. It offered easy access to an extraordinary number of fine cruising venues, as long as the planning took into account the stunning tidal differences, which can create vast stretches of beach where a few hours before was only water (see sidebar Cruising Tips).

The weather in early spring was stable and sunny and tem-

LADY JEANINE at anchor at Bahia Carricito south of San Carlos

peratures remained relatively cool. However, we did not take into account the hated northers that whistled down from the Four Corners every other week during the winter and early spring. As we found out the hard way, March was typically the windiest month of the year. The storms usually blew day and night for two to six days. In between, we were told, we could expect up to a week of decent sailing weather. Of course, during the next three or four weeks, we followed the weather report closely. But once a norther blew in, there really wasn't much we could do, except hole up in the marina, relax at the pool, wander the streets of San Carlos and Guaymas, the next town to the south, savor the seafood at the local cantina, and dance the nights away at Tequilas, a bar with live rock music in the marina.

Once the northers blew past, Martini Bay in San Carlos offered a practical point of departure to some of the finest sailing I have ever experienced. By late March, we were taking weeklong tours to Guaymas and solitary coves and to caletas in the vicinity with colorful names like Algadones, San Pedro, Carricito, Amarga, Venecia, Julio Villa, and Cocinas. Among our favorites was Caleta Amarga, a fairly tight little anchorage, very private, with a solitary wild palm tree and views of blazing sunsets that framed the homeward bound flocks of pelicans and seagulls every evening. We once spent three days there napping, beach combing, swimming in the emerald waters, and hiking among the magnificent giant cardon cactuses (pachycereus pringlei) that cover the nearby foothills. They are the world's largest cacti, older and taller than even the saguaro cactus (carnegiea gigantea) found in Arizona. The largest cardones can grow to a height of 70 feet and weigh up to 25 tons. They grow slowly and can live well over 300 years. They are something of a romantic oddity since they bloom only at night.

Another favorite area was Ensenada Julio Villa, bound by a white sandy beach and granite cliffs that offered protection against winds from all points of the compass, except the south. The place was named after Julio Villa, who used to fish the little cove with dynamite and met a grisly fate. He had tied a cluster of spares around his waist, and might have lit one of them by mistake. There was a tremendous bang, and when the nearby villagers arrived to investigate, most of Julio was gone, a victim of his own crude fishing method. All that was left to do was bury the remains that could be found and mark the site with a cross, which can be seen to this day at the west end of the beach.

Taking a walk in the clear shallows of the Cocinas beach, the author disturbs scores of tiny sting rays

Ensenada Las Cocinas, a lovely north-facing cove, was our northernmost anchorage, just south of the Midriff Islands. We rowed the dinghy ashore, searched the beach for shells, startled a covey of pelicans in the process, and listened to a raven's pandemonium on a distant rock. Armed with blanket and umbrella, Jeanine claimed a secluded section of this beach and spent the remainder of the afternoon in lazy tranquility, basking in the white, hot sands while the incoming tide lapped at her feet.

The sunset was spectacular, the Baja dust and the clouds to the west shimmering a billowing palette of auburn, purple and gold. That night we bobbed at our moorage and watched the colors of the sky until the sun dipped beneath the distant, dusty horizon, the ragged mountains on the peninsula were hardly visible, except for the hazy outline of the Three Virgins, the peaks north of Santa Rosalia.

The shores of the Baja peninsula beckoned, so Jeanine and I began to consider a crossing of the Gulf of California. We discussed our plans with the resident cruising veterans, who encouraged us to try it, suggesting that we wait until after the next norther had blown itself out. The recommended tactic was to head out into the gulf just after sunset, and motor across to Santa Rosalia at night. This would allow us to take advantage of the evening calms while putting us on the other side shortly after sunrise.

The next few days were an exercise in patience. After a couple of calm, sunny days, a mild norther kicked in and blew day and night for the next four days. On the morning of the fifth day the wind died and the gulf turned to glass, exactly as expected. We consulted with the old salts one more time and shortly before midnight we cast off and headed for open water, motoring at a little over 6 knots across a windless sea. The soft glow of our GPS screen and Orion's belt guided us to Santa Rosalia, while a chevron of bioluminescence bubbled from either side of our bow and left a long, glowing tail of green at our stern. Later that night, the moon rose at our backs to keep us company until dawn when we passed Tortuga Island and the outline of Santa Rosalia began to emerge from the mist on the western horizon.

The morning brought a northwesterly breeze, which was most welcome because, after so many hours of droning along under engine, we now could sail the last 15 miles to Santa Rosalia in peace and quiet. We doused our sails at the breakwater, started the motor once again, and worked our way to the battered remnant of a marina that still bore the signs of Hurricane Lester that had raided this area in 1992.

Ricardo, the marina manager, kindly helped us get settled and fired up the water boiler which allowed us to enjoy the luxury of a hot shower. He then drove us to town in his antique Chevy, so we could buy fuel and check in with the local officials. I could not help but chuckle at Jeanine who had the honor to ride upfront, next to Ricardo, perched on a chicken crate as we drove pell-mell through intersections and stop signs. Ricardo's Chevy, it became painfully obvious, had no brakes.

That night, we enjoyed a sumptuous Mexican dinner in a charming outdoor restaurant decorated with strings of multicolored lights. Later, we dawdled through the town, looked into stores and taquerias, made our way past a couple of crowded street-side bars, and took a moment to step inside the famous prefab metal church, Iglesia Santa Barbara, which was designed by Gustave Eiffel of Eiffel Tower fame.

Back out on the street, a gentleman with a Clark Gable mustache hailed me to inquire if I would like a haircut. It had been at least six weeks since my last trim, so my looks were beginning to resemble those of a castaway. Why not? He ushered me into a tiny shop, half learn-to, half woodshed with a barber chair that was at least half a century old and had ceramic arm rests and split leather upholstery. Power was provided with a thick yellow extension chord from the neighboring shop. For the next 45 minutes, he worked diligently, trimming, snipping, and humming. It must have been quite a show, because the two windows were crowded with the faces of curious onlookers who wanted to see a Yankee getting his hair cut. The barber's wife and child eventually came to watch, too. While Jeanine held the baby, they discussed the relative merits of my makeover. At last he was done. He passed me a cracked mirror, and, *¡hola!* a marine colonel stared back at me. The stubble left on my head wouldn't need a comb for at least two weeks. Later, we bought some animal figurines that were carved from ironwood. The merchant told us that this was the handiwork of the Sori Indians, who lived on Tiburon Island, farther north. Thus far, they have staunchly resisted efforts by the Mexican government to bring them into the mainstream and continue to refuse to work for anyone, instead choosing to support themselves with their beautiful carvings.

The next morning promised some fine sailing, so we left Santa Rosalia and headed south for Punta Chivato. Pushed by a following sea, LADY JEANINE ran through the boiling surf and in her wake the water's confused surface resembled a potato patch. Under full sail we ran past Isla Marcos, skirted the barrier shoals that extended from the island's southern shore before we gained deeper water where we jibed for Chivato. We spent the night at Playa Santa Inez, but didn't dwell for long, since our destination was Bahia Concepcion, a gorgeous emerald estuary farther south with fantastic views of Baja's desert mountains and countless solitary coves. We passed a series of smaller estuaries in a freshening desert breeze that eventually forced us to furl away half of the jib. Soon after passing the town of Mulege we entered the great bay and I spied some tiny fishing hamlets on the eastern shore. Finally, with daylight and wind fading, we found a tiny anchorage snug against the cliffs of a small island named Isla Coyote. I set two anchors fore and aft, with a pair of hawks staring fiercely down on us, occasionally breaking the majestic silence with their screams.

We spent the last hours transfixed by a gorgeous sunset in azure and pink, while LADY JEANINE lazily bobbed in the

Pilot whales are a common sight in Bahia Concepcion

swells. Just below our keel, a school of tiny fish swam to and fro in perfect formation as if choreographed for a staged water ballet. That night, with the rising of the moon and Ursa Major hanging in the sky to the north, we once more felt like being adrift toward the infinite. The long gulf crossing paid big dividends: We had found our slice of paradise in a land of sharp and austere beauty with emerald waters, hidden coves and estuaries, and silent, lonely beaches. Some might consider Baja a massive, barren peninsula. John Steinbeck wrote that humans were not much wanted here, and one early Jesuit missionary even described it as nothing more than a pathless waste between two oceans. But nothing could be farther from the truth. This peninsula is very much alive, especially its shores and offshore waters that are home to thousands of invertebrates, several species of whales and dolphins, and about 900 species of fish.

Baja is part of the infamous San Andreas fault, the tail end of a mountain range that begins thousands of miles north in the Aleutians. About 20 million years ago, the fault opened a chasm in the earth's crust that was more than 10,000 feet deep and separated the peninsula from the mainland. The resulting isolation and the need for creatures to adapt to the desert climate has resulted in a good deal of freakishness—scientists call it *endemism*—of flora and fauna. Here you'll find plants that crawl, rattle snakes without rattles, rats that jump like kangaroos, toads that live almost exclusively underground in a near death state, and a giant lizard that stores water in built-in sacks and gurgles when it walks.

After a night at Isla Coyote, we headed across the channel to Playa Santa Barbara, a shallow north-facing cove fringed by wild palms and bordered by an exquisite white, sandy beach. As we headed south, the water suddenly turned smooth as mercury, the sails went limp as the breeze suddenly shut off, forcing us to motor the last quarter of a mile into the bay. We paddled ashore in the inflatable, built a camp in the shade of the wild palms and luxuriated in solitude for the rest of the afternoon. That night, I broke out the last of the steaks while Jeanine sliced the last of our tomatoes. We ate on deck, listened to one of our favorite albums, while LADY JEANINE swung gently at anchor until the sun disappeared in an azure ribbon beyond the sawtooth mountains. We stayed here for three days before heading back north to Playa Concepcion, and anchored in a beautiful expanse of a cove, with two natural hot springs and a row of summer homes. We stayed for a couple of days, sampled the pleasures of the springs, which were cooled twice daily by the incoming tide, wandered the beach, and visited with some fellow gypsies from South Africa on a Westsail 42, a wild Irishman and an Englishman who were circumnavigating on a steel ketch. They had bickered all the way across the Atlantic and through the Panama Canal. I confided to Jeanine that I wondered how they could possibly make it to Hawaii without killing each other. Two days later, we tacked north to Bahia Santo Domingo, a remarkably shallow bay with an exquisite view west and north and miles of open, white sandy beach. From there, we sailed north to Punta Chivato to prepare for our return crossing to San Carlos.

That night, we lay in our berth and looked up at the stars and the moon for a long time before falling asleep. There was no question, enduring the long drive, sitting out the hated northers, braving the peculiarities of Mexican highways and slogging across the Gulf of California for 14 hours had been well worth the effort. Of course, the trip was not quite as planned or expected, nor could it have been. But this is a wilderness, unpredictable, complex and solitary, rough and incredibly beautiful, a place where water, sky and desert meet in perfect harmony. Looking back on this trip, I realized that this journey was not simply taking us to the fringe of the desert and across an expanse of water, but deep into our soul. Yes, there were surprises and some unexpected turns, but through them we were given the opportunity to experience the gracious warmth and hospitality of the Mexican people, the mystery of the sea and the beauty of this wild and barren land. Indeed, we were more than sufficiently compensated for our troubles. But there was one more adventure in store.

Storm Crossing

Our sentimental farewell from Baja didn't last long. It came to a quick and brutal end in a storm that hit 36 hours earlier than forecast just as we were crossing the open water of the Gulf from Punta Chivato to San Carlos. It was the ultimate test in resilience and seamanship that forced us to use every resource at our command to survive. Before heading out we believed that a 36-hour window was sufficient for an 85-mile crossing. Besides, provisions were running low and we had less than a week's time left to make it back to San Carlos, haul out and drive back to Colorado. We anchored near Playa Santa Inez, just west of Punta Chivato when we learned that a fast-moving low was barreling down on us from the Pacific, but it wasn't expected to hit this area until a day and a half later. Two neighboring boats were planning to clear out and make the run for the mainland that evening. A nearby shrimper also planned to get out and advised us to do the same, suggesting that we might encounter relatively flat seas if we left early that evening. I discussed the matter with Jeanine, and we agreed to leave for San Carlos.

At about 4:30 p.m., we weighed anchor and headed out into the Gulf. Before sunset we passed between Punta Chivato and Islas Santa Inez, and turned northeast toward San Carlos. We had no way of knowing that the approaching front had merged with a massive low-pressure system off the coast of Southern California and was diverted southeast by a ridge of high pressure in the Four Corners. It was passing over the Peninsular range at the time we left Punta Chivato and it was about to strike San Carlos and the middle gulf sometime after midnight.

Shortly after sunset the seas began to build, and the wind freshened to 15 knots with gusts to 20 knots. I had already double-reefed the main, hoping that this was only a stiff evening breeze that would die in an hour or two. We motor-sailed and made better than 6 knots, which in my estimation was more than we could have managed under sail alone. As dusk faded at our stern, the waves crested at five feet, and the wind continued to increase. Jeanine and I discussed our options, and found it pointless to turn back. We would have been forced to bash through a breaking surf for more than 15 miles and I was deeply concerned about passing between Punta Chivato and Islas Santa Inez in the dark. Even in broad daylight it was a tricky affair, but in the dark without any navigation lights, it could turn into a catastrophe. A half hour later, we overheard two other boats in the area talking on the radio, saying they "felt sorry for that small boat behind us— they're really in for it." I looked at Jeanine as we banged our way toward San Carlos. They meant us. A little later, we raised them on the VHF and another boat, a ketch named CIRCE, which had picked up a weather report. She relayed that the isobars behind us were much more clustered than originally predicted, and we could expect winds of at least 7 on the Beaufort scale (28–33 knots) within a few hours. She then altered course and headed north to make San Carlos on a reach. We made our last contact with CIRCE just as she disappeared over the horizon and we were getting badly pounded. Intermittently I could see her stern light flickering in the distance ahead, as we topped a swell before dropping down into the next trough. We wished them Godspeed and a safe journey and they returned the favor. I decided to get rid of the main entirely and secured it with shock cords. I hoped this would free me enough to pay full attention to the engine and the helm. By 11 p.m. it had gotten very cold, and the seas continued to build to a considerable height. The wind meter indicated gusts of 35 to 40 knots apparent and later I found out that the waves had reached heights from 8 to 13 feet. I clipped my tether to a nearby cleat and wedged myself against the cockpit coaming by locking my knee against the starboard bench. It wasn't the most comfortable of positions but, unfortunately, I would be forced to endure it throughout most of the next ten hours.

Jeanine had inserted two of the companionway hatch boards and gone below, which reduced the communication between us to a minimum. She monitored the radio and suggested coffee, but I declined since most of it would have been spilled in the pounding. She offered a snack, additional sweaters and another parka, but I was concerned she might lose her balance and fall if she left her berth. The Gulf of California is notorious for square waves that have a short fetch, steep crests and narrow troughs, and a tendency to break prematurely. I could hear a loud rushing sound as each breaking wave bore down on us. In most cases, I chose not to look back. I was busy enough without twisting my head to watch row upon row of white-capped, foaming rogues descend on us. Still, the largest waves loomed high above deck and shimmered with bioluminescence that I could not help but watch out of the corner of my eye. Sometimes they missed us, but at other times we took a direct hit, which forced me to alter course so I could slide obliquely off the crest rather than surf wildly straight down into the troughs and risk pitch poling. Sometimes, I was also forced to pull back the throttle to reset a cavitating prop, while the boat rolled wildly and turned broadside to the wind. The cabin was a mess. Books, dishes, cushions, and bed covers were strewn everywhere. The porta-potti had broken loose, but luckily, it didn't spill the contents of the holding tank, so we were lucky in that respect. Clothing, PFDs, tethers, and charts were scattered on the cabin sole. To minimize spillover from the winch hole of the keel's hoisting mechanism, Jeanine had stuffed towels into the opening, so we were not too concerned about taking on water. It was only a small comfort, however. I checked our inflatable, which I chose to tow, reasoning that if we should founder, it would be readily accessible instead of stowed on the foredeck. In a worst-case scenario, I would not have time to untie it and toss into the water. Sometimes, it nearly passed us, sometimes it jerked wildly back and forth like a fish on a hook. Still, a quick check with the flashlight proved that it was secure and it hadn't shipped more than an inch or two of water. At the worst of times that night, our little boat under bare poles must have been a doleful sight: tilting, yawing and lurching wildly from side to side, her scuppers desperately trying to keep up with water that poured into the cockpit, her lee rail dipping and scooping up the sea only to empty again as she surfed and pounded through the mounting surge. Our

GPS was unable to obtain a fix, most likely because of all the lurching and tossing. I tried to reset it, but it went out within minutes. On the third try, it managed to track our position for about ten minutes before it lost contact to the orbiting satellites. At this point, I set it just long enough to get a fix on the stars, checked my compass heading, unplugged it, and tossed it to Jeanine so it would not be washed overboard. I also wondered about the other two boats and the shrimper. I never learned whether CIRCE also decided to proceed under engine alone, in the hope of escaping the worst of the storm. The other boat, HARMONY, continued to try to raise us, but was forced to drop her main and make her way northeast with a smaller headsail and her mizzen. We were burning about a gallon of gas every fifty minutes. About four and a half hours after we had left Punta Chivato, I had managed to crawl forward, open the starboard hatch, and switch the fuel line from the large tank to the small one. However, at the rate we were going, I knew I was going to have to refill the larger tank from our spare jugs. I would have to put the engine in neutral and let LADY JEANINE drift broadside to the waves while trying to pour the gas with a minimum of spillage. At 1 a.m. it was impossible to wait any longer. Jeanine braced herself in the hatch opening and grabbed the flashlight. I put the motor in neutral, pulled the main tank out of the starboard bench, and had her shine the flashlight on the tank while I removed the cap and refilled it from two auxiliary jugs. I managed to fill the tank, but not before spilling at least a gallon of gas onto the self-draining cockpit floor and on my shoes. I dropped the tank back into the hold and switched over the gas line without a breach and without having the boat twist out of control. We were now good for at least another 4 hours. I rinsed the cockpit with a gallon jug of drinking water and emptied another on my shoes and over my hands.

I crawled back to the wheel, wedged myself back into my position on the port bench, put the engine in gear, and pushed the throttle forward. To my horror the engine barely responded. A quick check of the throttle mechanism revealed a split cable casing. Now, I had another problem to worry about, one that called for an immediate fix. I carefully wrapped the casing with heavy electric tape and gently pushed the throttle forward. The engine gradually came to life, sped up and pushed us forward, closer to San Carlos at nearly 6 knots.

By 2 a.m. we had covered more than half the distance across, and I nurtured some hope that conditions were not going to get much worse. I had heard that the gulf could generate waves of 40 feet or more, given the right conditions and a long fetch, but for my own sanity, I had put the thought out of my head. My primary responsibility was to stay focused, steer through each wave, one at a time, and keep us on course. Shortly before 5 a.m., I discerned the faint, sweeping glow of the light at Punta Haro, 20 miles south of San Carlos. As we continued to pound east, the glow gradually became brighter until the light appeared and flashed in steady three-second intervals. Soon after that, the lights of Guaymas began to shimmer on the horizon, more promise that landfall was approaching. Finally, at dawn, I saw the mainland's coast for the first time and the distinct outline of Las Tetas de Cabra (a mountain that some people think deserves a more romantic name). I topped off our main tank one more time from our spare fuel supply to make sure we were fully prepared for the final portion of this wild ride. As I recapped the jugs, the morning light revealed the true magnitude and force of the seas behind us. We were surrounded by breakers that cascaded down on us. Perhaps it had been better that I had not seen how bad it was as we made our way across the gulf that night. But now with the day dawning and safe harbor in sight, I felt that we were able to handle whatever nature might throw at us. I put the engine in gear and turned off the running lights. Two hours later, we cleared Punta Doble and turned north into Bahia San Carlos, toward our berth. Later, I was to talk with the skipper of HARMONY who confirmed that we had battled waves as high as 13 feet and winds up to 45 knots and that we had indeed ridden the cusp of a storm that was to wreak havoc up and down the Gulf of California for the next few days. Much to our dismay we heard that three boats on the Pacific side of Baja had suffered serious damage. One sailor had to be airlifted, and the other two were holed up and anchored in five-foot swells at Laguna San Ignacio.

We hadn't slept for nearly thirty hours, but the crossing had left us emotionally drained, yet full of adrenalin, so we found it hard to settle down. We napped fitfully for a couple of hours, showered, and had breakfast at the hotel. Later that afternoon, we drove up to the scenic overlook at Caleta Lalo and, for a very long and quiet moment, looked westward over the great expanse of the gulf. The wind was still blowing hard and the sea was a chaos of foaming waves as far as the eye could see. I looked at Jeanine and squeezed her hand. She looked west for an instant and turned away, but I was transfixed. It was hard to believe that we had come through that hell in a small trailerable sailboat and survived unscathed.

I realized that we had been seriously tested, but that we also had been very lucky. Certainly, our little boat had been through the very worst that night and I could not help but wonder if we hadn't fared better if I had stayed with the double-reefed main as the storm began to build, or at the very least, with the jib unfurled to about a quarter of its full size. But what if we still had to refuel? That could have posed a serious problem, since the boat would have been even more out of control with no one at the helm. In hindsight, I think that a 36-hour window might not be sufficient for an 85-mile crossing on a small boat with some safety margin. If faced with the same situation again, I would certainly return to a secure anchorage, wait out the next four days, and thoroughly check the weather before making a final decision to cross.

This experience now makes me think twice about crossing open water in such a small boat when there is any potential for bad weather, although most of the locals who owned trailerable boats told me that it was routine to wait for a window before making the crossing to Punta Chivato, regardless of the time of the year. I remain convinced however, that impatience and rushing things in marginal conditions are two major causes for accidents and loss of life. Still, in the final analysis, I suppose that the proof of our abilities and the success of this journey lay in the result. Though somewhat shaken, Jeanine and I had survived without injury and our boat came out intact, except that it might have been a bit saltier now.

Within three days, we were fully rested and making plans for a three-day tour down the coast. I'm resigned to the fact that we probably never will get enough of sailing. We realize that we are taking certain risks anytime we leave terra firma behind in a small boat. But next time we decide to cross (if we do it at all), we'll go later in the year when the likelihood to encounter a norther on the way is much smaller.

The Gulf of California:
Cruising Tips for Trailer Sailors

Getting there: Take I-19 south to Nogales, Arizona, which connects to a divided Mexican toll road that will take you to San Carlos or as far south as Mazatlan. Be aware that Mexican highways are a good deal narrower than American roads, and the backwash from passing trucks may be dangerous to your rig if you are not prepared for the blast. You should also recognize that Mexicans drive "somewhat differently" than in the United States, so be alert and prepared to take quick evasive action. Watch the fuel gauge because Mexican gas stations (government-owned Pemex) are not nearly as frequent as U.S. filling stations. Teenage boys, emulating New York's squeegee men, may attempt to wash your windshield at intersections and stop signs. If you have no interest in such services, politely say "No, no," and gently wave them off. If you choose to cruise the Mexican Highway I on the Baja side you'll get down to Cabo San Lucas. Eventually. These are hard-earned miles, because it still is a narrow, winding, two-lane road with very few filling stations.

Although opinions vary, most experienced trailer boaters would discourage driving at night in Mexico. Most gas stations are closed, unfenced livestock tends to wander across the highway. These animals are difficult to spot in the dark and there is an element of surprise, since warning signs are nowhere to be found. Blind curves and speed bumps come your way unannounced and may force sudden corrections on your part that could make you lose control of your rig, especially if you are speeding. To cross the border, you will need a passport, proof of Mexican insurance, and a temporary import permit for your towing vehicle, boat, and trailer.

Charts we used: We had no luck finding any reliable official charts so we used cruising guides and local knowledge to plan our trips. We found Gerry Cunningham's guides very useful (Cruising Guide to Middle Gulf, 3rd edition, Cruising Guide to San Carlos, 4th edition) because informal charts were included, www.gerrycruise.com. Another source was Fish'n'Map, Sea of Cortez—North and Sea of Cortez—South, www.fishnmap.com. Another site you might find useful is www.cruisecortez.com , which offers a simple map of the San Carlos region www.cruisecortez .com/sancarloscruisingarea.htm and a number of guide books that appeal to novices and seasoned salts alike: www.cruisecortez.com/resources.htm

Finding a moorage: The best trailer sailing is south of the Midriff Islands. Marina Seca in San Carlos on the mainland will rent a slip at very reasonable rates, and you may store your trailer in their boat yard at a nominal cost. Marina Seca Phone: (+52 622) 22-61230, (+52-622) 22-61202, (888) 499-5513, www.marinasancarlos.com/seca.html

Your towing vehicle may be parked almost indefinitely near your slip for easy access to shopping and showers.

Hotel amenities, including the hotel pool and beach, are included with all slip rentals. The marina can launch your boat with a hoist for a nominal fee (don't forget to tip the workmen). This is the preferred alternative for most trailer boaters, since the Sea of Cortez is exceptionally salty and can play havoc with your trailer and towing vehicle, unless they are rinsed thoroughly and immediately.

Provisioning: Since marinas and fuel docks are widely scattered, carry extra fuel for extended trips and bring plenty of bottled water. If you want fresh produce, buy only fruit that you can peel at the mercados, and do not store cold food where it is in direct contact with your ice, since the ice is typically made of unprocessed water. Block ice can be bought at most liquor stores and on the waterfront in Guaymas. Most packaged and canned foods cost one third or even 50 percent less than in the U.S. Do not hesitate to ask snowbirds, retirees and veteran cruisers for advice. They know the best places to eat and shop from personal experience.

Although a good many Mexicans know a bit of English, try to learn a bit of "survival" Spanish and use it whenever possible. Also, the Mexicans are a very gracious and congenial people and usually appreciate any effort to learn their language, no matter how clumsy—an excellent way to make friends is to ask for the Spanish word for something.

Navigation: At the very least, you should have a GPS, a depth finder, VHF (to stay in touch with the local cruising networks), a cruising guide (See "Suggested Additional Reading—Mexico") and local charts, which are somewhat primitive, although Gerry Cunningham has provided an excellent cruising guide with waypoints and accompanying maps, and Charlie's Charts are reasonably accurate. We found that sailing here requires good dead-reckoning skills, and that one could make due without electronic gadgets such chart plotter, radar, autopilot, or Single Sideband Radio. Browse www.cruisecortez.com or Web sites and blogs that are being put up by other cruisers. Be careful though, and remember that you use the posted information at your own risk. Most of these sites reflect individual experiences and are not professionally edited for clarity or vetted for accuracy.

The Gulf of California is notorious for steep, breaking waves, narrow troughs, and sudden storms. If you are cruising the mainland, you may want to limit your itinerary to venues north of Guaymas and south of the Midriff Islands, but watch the tide. If you choose to cross over to Baja, make sure that you have at least a 36-hour weather window.

Tides: You will be in for big surprises and possibly a night on the hard, if you don't account for the tidal differences, especially in the northern portions of the gulf. The Marine Discovery Web site of the University of Arizona http://marinediscovery.arizona.edu/gulf.html explains this phenomenon: "The Gulf of California is one of the youngest ocean bodies, probably having been formed by the separation of the North American Plate and the Pacific Plate by plate tectonic movement. It has mixed semi-diurnal tides and one of the greatest tidal ranges on earth. The difference between the highest tide and lowest tide covers up to 2 miles horizontally and as much as 9 meters [27feet] vertically in the northern gulf."

Weather: The weather on the Sea of Cortez is influenced by the desert climate and can be subject to violent swings. During our springtime trip we had to hunker down frequently and let the northers blow by. These are fierce north winds, which originate in the Four Corners and can exceed 40 knots and generate turbulent seas that can easily be as high as five or 10 feet, sometimes higher. Northers commonly last four or five days and are followed by several days of calmer sailing weather. During summer, temperatures on the Baja peninsula are extremely hot and pesky insects are a constant problem. Hurricane season lasts from July to September and usually affects the areas south of San Carlos or Santa Rosalia, although there are notable exceptions, such as Hurricane Lester in 1992.

The quickest route across the Sea of Cortez is from San Carlos to Punta Chivato, a distance of about 90 nautical miles. Plan a night crossing, so you will arrive at the other side at dawn of the following day. Do not put yourself in a position to arrive at a strange port in the dark. Mexican navigational aids are minimal at best and not all shoals and landfalls are noted on the charts.

Anchoring: Carry good ground tackle, since you will be anchoring most of the time once you have left San Carlos. You should carry an 18-20 pound Danforth and a plow anchor of some sort on 10-15 feet of chain and 250 to 300 feet of ⅜- to half-inch triple-strand nylon rode. Unfortunately, pump-out stations still are far and few between on the Gulf of California, simply because the infrastructure is not in place. Until this changes you either have to use a porta-potti with a large holding tank or you have to go out at least two miles before dumping.

Thoughts about Voyaging

For all that happened that terrible night we crossed the Gulf of California, there's something exquisite and beautiful about sailing in these parts of Mexico. Even a few years later, we fondly remember sunsets that swept the sea with pink and gold, the starry night on a windless gulf during our outbound crossing to Baja, pelicans that followed our boat as if tethered to a kite string, the idyllic, hidden anchorages and rummaging the shore for sea shells while the waves flung pebbles at our feet.

The culture, the ambience and the people who are a part of this venue as much as the sea and the wind cast a spell that worked its magic on us: a guitar that echoed down a village street late at night, a lone fisherman singing to himself as he worked the shoals off San Pedro Bay, curtains billowing from a tiny adobe cottage at the edge of the sea; the sacral music that echoed from a crowded cathedral on a brilliant Sunday morning; an elderly woman cooking tortillas near the chapel square; a small, flower-covered altar facing the sea.

But during this Baja sojourn, we also found something deeply personal that was almost impossible to grasp at first. But gradually and almost imperceptibly we fell into the charm of the Mexican cruising life. Home was wherever we dropped the hook. We could go anywhere we wanted, do as we wanted, and stay as long as we wanted. If we chose, we could hoist sail and chase the sun over the horizon until it fell into the sea, or we could find our own personal sanctuary in the solitary lee of a tiny island with a beach as pure and white as the snow in the Rocky Mountains of Colorado.

Walt Whitman once wrote how he had loafed at his ease, observing a spear of summer grass. We too had time to loaf at our ease, contemplating the rising moon and observing the glittering water in our wake; tracking the gleam of a lighthouse that was piercing the darkness; or spending all day under sail, in the steady rock and sway of the sea while listening to the constant, hypnotic swish of the waves moving past the hull. To us this was about as close as we might come to finding perfection in this world.

There will always be something incomprehensible and mystical about sailing and our connection with the sea. Like Ishmael, Herman Melville's protagonist in *Moby Dick* and his dockside philosophers, Jeanine and I know when it's time for us to escape civilization and run away to the sea. When we are on the water, we can revel among fellow sailors, celebrate freedom, and adopt the perspective of prophets and sages to examine the depths of our wandering souls and our place in the universe. Given just the right time and place, we might turn into happy castaways, disciples of the wind, barefoot, barely clothed, our tanned and salty skin turning amber in the afternoon sun. While that's a rare moment of grace, it is worth the search.

By hoisting sail, Jeanine and I are privileged to experience the closest possible relation with each other, often in places of exquisite beauty where we can escape from the daily grind and the burden of responsibility. In the solitude of secluded and tranquil coves we watch the sunset with reverence or marvel at the beauty and the power of the sea, as we try to understand the wonderful mystery of life's force deep within ourselves.

To us there's no better way to celebrate life than under sail.

Appendix I

Boat Specifications & Web sites

Chrysler Man O'War
- LOA: 15'0"
- LWL: 13'5"
- Beam: 5'4"
- Displacement: 195 lbs.
- Draft: 2'7"
- Sail area: 85 sq.ft.
- Designer: J.R. Macalpine-Downie
  http://chryslersailing.lizards.net/manowar.html

Victoria 18
- LOA: 18'6"
- LWL: 12'6"
- Beam: 5'6"
- Displacement: 1,250 lb.
- Ballast: 560 lb.
- Draft: 2'0"

- Sail area: 163 sq. ft
- Designers: William and George McVay
  www.victoriayachts.com/vicsite/index.html

MacGregor Venture 22

- LOA 22'0"
- LWL 18'2"
- Beam 7'
- Draft (keel up/down) 1'/ 5' 6"
- Displacement 1,700 lb.
- Ballast 500 lb.
- Sail Area 175 sq. ft.
- Designer: George MacGregor
  http://macgregorowners.com/
  http://members.aol.com/tralrsailr/toc.html
  www.tompatterson.com/Sailing/webring/webring.html
  http://bbs.trailersailor.com/forums/macgregor/index.cgi

Balboa 26

- LOA: 25'7"
- LWL: 20'10"
- Beam: 8'0"
- Draft (keel up/down): 1'10"/ 5'0"
- Displacement: 3,600 lb.
- Ballast: 1,200 lb.
- Sail area: 293 sq. ft.
- Designer: Lyle C. Hess
  www.practical-sailor.com/boatreviews/Balboa-26-boat-review.html
  http://cliffunruh.com/balboa26.htm
  http://groups.yahoo.com/group/balboa26-boats/

Appendix II

Why Trailer Sail

Why slog along for hundreds or thousands of miles at 5 knots per hour, possibly hiring a delivery crew to do it for you while you have to earn the money, when you can do more than 50 on the freeway? Trailer sailing, I'm convinced, is the only way of enjoying a variety of cruising venues affordably and on your own keel. For the past two decades, we have trailered our Balboa 26 over 25,000 miles throughout the western United States (that was after we graduated from our smaller boats), to sail in places like the Pacific Northwest, the lakes in the Rocky Mountains, Lake Powell in the southwest desert, the coast of Southern California, and the Gulf of California in Mexico. Next, we are planning to visit the East Coast. But instead of transiting the Panama Canal, we'll simply hitch up and follow a southeast heading to Florida, along Interstates 25 and 10.

But there's another advantage to cruising on a trailerable boat: If we choose, we can do a one-way trip, meaning the destination that's farthest downwind. So instead of doing a short loop, we can do a much longer one-way, catch a ride back to the starting point, fetch truck and trailer that are hopefully still parked there and drive back to pick up the boat before heading home.

Of course, we have to be a little selective when choosing cruising venues and consider the limitations of our own abilities and those of the boat. While it is possible to buy a bluewater-capable trailer yacht like a Pacific Seacraft Flicka or Dana 24, or one of the larger Com-Pac models, most trailerable sailboats were not designed to cross oceans, but for operation in near-shore venues or on lakes. Hence, we never had any interest in offshore cruising, or in places with few ports of refuge. If money is tight, you could follow the example of some of our budget-minded cruising friends who use their boat as a camper en route to their cruising destinations.

Expenses and upgrades: A new trailerable sailboat in the 24- to 26-foot range, costs somewhere between $25,000 and $50,000, including trailer and sails. Pre-owned, pocket cruisers run between $8,000 and $30,000, depending on age, condition, and amenities. We found that late-model trailerable cruisers tend to be in much better condition than "vintage" boats that might have sat around neglected for years. In general, boats that have been stored on the hard and have received proper care, suffer less from corrosion, osmosis, strain, and wear than vessels that are moored or docked for most or all of the year. On such boats there is no need to hire a diver to scrub the hull, replace zincs, complete underwater repairs, or check thru-hulls. Besides, dry storage costs only a fraction of slip fees and if you have a large enough property and friendly neighbors, you might even consider storing the boat in your driveway or backyard. In this case the only mooring expenses you encounter will come at a port of call or marina while cruising. Trailer sailors save at the beginning and the end of their trips too, because they don't have to pay a crane or Travelift operator ($300 per hour and up) to launch and retrieve their boat. Instead, a modest fee for using the launch ramp is all they have to pay. There are exceptions to this rule, however. For venues with very salty water such as the Gulf of California, I recommend launching by crane or Travelift to avoid exposing truck and trailer to the corrosive effects of the seawater, which reduces maintenance, wear and tear.

The truck: Of course, these calculations do not account for the cost of a towing vehicle, which should be capable of pulling a trailer load between 4,000 and 8,000 pounds, meaning the gross weight of trailer and the fully equipped boat. For example, our Balboa 26 has a factory weight of 3,500 pounds. However, boat and trailer actually weigh a little less than 7,000 pounds, including our gear, engine, ground tackle, provisions, and sails. We live in mountainous country where passes of 10,000 feet and more in altitude above sea level are common. Therefore we needed a vehicle with some muscle and chose a ¾-ton Chevrolet pick-up truck with a 410 rear end, a standard transmission, and an engine that generates a little over 400 hp (see Appendix IV, "Tips for Towing"). The truck is factory-certified to tow a little over 7,000 pounds. In our case a lesser capacity would be detrimental, even impossible. Sure, diesel engines have more torque and are better for towing, but they are also quite expensive, more difficult to repair—especially if an injector needs to be replaced—and I have very little experience in diesel engine maintenance. Besides, not all gas stations have a diesel pump.

In calculating the expense of a trailer, it is important to account for repairs and replacements, including wiring and lights, which are subject to corrosion because of immersion, if you still use the old-style incandescent bulbs, and trailer tires, which suffer from heavy loads and exposure to UV light, especially in the southwest summer. Replacing incandescent bulbs with a water-proof LED lighting system will take care of most electrical troubles and covering the tires when the trailer is not in use helps extend their useful life. Insurance costs may also be somewhat higher, since coverage should include mishaps on the water *and* on the road when the accident risk is greatest.

Gas mileage is also a consideration for planning trips. Towing several thousand pounds with a half- or three-quarter ton truck is not going to win any prize for fuel efficiency. Depending on engine size, you might not get more than 12 to 15 miles per gallon, so a 500-mile roundtrip requires anywhere between 34 and 42 gallons of fuel. Add to that the gasoline for the auxiliary engine, in our case a 9.9-horsepower outboard that burns about one gallon per hour at 6 to 7 knots.

All boats require regular maintenance and trailer yachts are no different. However, this is a relatively simple task and won't strain your budget too badly. For example, most modern outboard motors can be winterized in less than ten minutes. Brightwork, which is relatively scarce on most modern trailerable boats, may need refinishing only every two or three years, and a wax job in spring will protect the gelcoat for most of the season. If your cruising includes night passages, double-check all electrical connections and running lights. The good news is that wiring and lights on the mast can be examined with ease when the mast is unstepped. Bottom paint, if you need any at all, also lasts much longer on a trailer boat, as long as you use a product that is specially formulated for dry storage. Consult with an expert, a paint manufacturer or some veteran trailer sailor to learn what works best.

The trailer, on the other hand, will need your attention more frequently, because nothing can ruin a vacation like a busted bearing, a blown tire or a light system that has gone mad. Preventive maintenance spares (bulbs, fuses, bearings and tire) minimize the stress that comes from having to hunt down a critical part in a remote place. Lights, bearings, and brakes should be serviced once a year, and replaced *before* they fail. This is a relatively simple task and can be done by anyone with a reasonable aptitude for mechanics. See Appendix V "Shaking down the Trailer".

A simple way to extend the useful life of your sails is to rinse and dry them and roll them up before storing them in a dry, cool and dark place in your house. Make it a habit to inspect running and standing rigging and replace parts that look worn or corroded. Lines and wires usually fail when they are under high load (e.g. when you sail in a stiff breeze and the boat is bashing into steep waves), which typically is the time when you can least afford breakage. Modern synthetic lines are susceptible to UV damage, so take them off when the boat is not in use or keep them covered.

Safety and enjoyment: Trailerable cruising boats have another often-overlooked advantage: They are small, simple and responsive enough for single-handed sailing. If you know your own limits and those of the vessel, these boats are absolutely safe and so much fun to sail that it makes owners of larger and more cumbersome vessels green with envy. In addition, smaller boats that are sailed on lakes or in protected venues close to shore can get outside help fast if it is absolutely necessary. Because everything on a small boat is smaller and lighter, damage is less likely to occur, and if it does, it tends to be less catastrophic than on a big boat. For example: Many modern trailerable sailboats have a retractable keel, therefore groundings are often less serious. If there is no major damage to the appendages or the hull, all it might take is starting the motor, cranking up the keel, and backing away from the trouble spot. Trailerable boats also have smaller sails. They are cheaper to buy, replace and maintain and they are much less difficult to handle, so it is easier to reef them in high winds.

If and when systems on larger boats fail, the costs and consequences can be dramatic. A broken 27-foot mast is annoying, but that pales compared to a 70-foot mast that can come down with enough force to cause serious injury or even death. By the same token, large built-in engines are costly to service or repair; cooling systems may clog or corrode and defective thru-hulls can sink a boat. A problem in the complex electrical installation can cause major headaches and we all heard about explosions that were caused by an electrical spark and a leaky propane line or tank.

To analyze the maintenance requirements of a larger boat, we only have to look at our other vessel, a Mariner 31 bluewater ketch that is moored at Long Beach, California. She must be hauled out and serviced at considerable cost at least every three years. She'll go just about anywhere, but when she doesn't, we still must pay monthly slip fees and insurance, service her engine, refinish her bottom and keep a constant eye on her rigging, hardware and electronics. Because she lives in a saltwater environment, she is much more susceptible to corrosion and wear, plus her topsides and brightwork require constant attention.

On the other hand, trailer sailors have to deal with issues that are unique to highway travel. A boat in tow is capable of dangerous escapades, if the trailer is poorly balanced, resulting in a whiplash effect. Towing a boat at excessive speed could prove catastrophic if the driver swerves, overcorrects, or needs to come to a sudden stop. If an overheated tire explodes at the wrong time, it may result in a loss of control and a major accident (See Appendix IV, "Tips for Towing"). A trailer that separates from the towing vehicle is almost a guarantee for disaster. I know of one trailer boater who looked to his right as he descended a hill and realized that the vehicle that passed him was his own boat that had broken loose from its hitch. It is also important to remember that stopping distance is almost tripled for a vehicle that tows a heavy trailer.

You will derive the greatest pleasure from trailer boating if you match your interests and cruising style with a boat that fits your budget and personal preferences. For example, if you plan to do most of your cruising in warmer climates, you should consider a boat with good air circulation and plenty of hatches, while frequent visits to colder climates would dictate a boat with a cozy cabin and a heater. Will you sail in high winds and rough waters or mostly on placid lakes? Do you want speed or safety, quick response or stability, creature comfort or a light and Spartan interior? If you plan to cruise by yourself often, the boat needs to be set up for singlehanded launching and sailing. Also think about the power and reliability of the auxiliary engine. Can it handle the conditions of the venues you plan to cruise? Is it strong enough to push the boat against a current, through high winds and steep waves?

Ask yourself about the onboard amenities, available headroom, storage space, creature comforts, aesthetic appeal, bunk size, and the functionality of the galley. Do you want an enclosed head or can you live with a porta-potti under the V-berth? Another factor is the size of the crew or the number of guests you plan on sailing with and the length of your cruises.

Despite certain limitations, compared to larger boats, a carefully selected trailerable cruising boat is a mighty attractive choice to safely explore different sailing venues on your own keel and have a good time while doing it, all without breaking the bank. To me these are plenty of good reasons to consider owning a fine little boat that sails well and isn't afraid to go on the road.

Appendix III

Sailing Well and Living Well

Only the uninformed would think that trailer sailors are a sorry lot, subsisting on granola bars and bottled water for days and even weeks on end. Nothing could be farther from the truth. The majority of 22- to 28-foot trailer boats provide reasonable living quarters and storage space that will meet your needs quite nicely, as long as you plan carefully.

Food: Preserving ice and perishable food is probably the biggest problem on a trailerboat. Aboard our Balboa 26, ice typically lasts five to eight days in hot weather in one of the new, highly insulated ice chests. It hardly lasts more than ten days, even if the chests are sealed and we are cruising in cool weather. Jeanine prefers to bring three smaller coolers rather than a single large one, because smaller coolers can be stowed more easily without exposure to warm, outside air, and they can remain sealed until their contents are needed. A friend of ours with a large family stores a whole day's provisions in a

Study your cruising guides and charts carefully before embarking

16-quart Styrofoam cooler. She brings as many coolers as there are days on her sailing itinerary.

We make ice for the cooler in gallon-sized plastic containers (milk jugs have a slight aftertaste). As the ice melts, we have cold drinking water. Ice containers covered with dry ice will last longer, but this requires separating the dry ice from the water ice with a towel or thick cloth.

We freeze almost all meat and cheese in Ziploc bags and store the meat in a separate cooler to avoid contamination of other foods if the meat thaws. We avoid mushy fruits like peaches, apricots, pears, and bananas that easily spoil. We store fruits and vegetables in plastic buckets and containers near the waterline where the temperature remains relatively cool. We don't bring cardboard boxes and paper bags, be-

Team up with your partner and plan your route carefully before departure

cause bugs might move aboard with them and we seal bread, sweets, syrup, and sugar in plastic bags. To simplify shopping, we keep a supply of canned foods aboard and restock it as needed. Our meals are simple, but we try to make them wholesome and tasty, sometimes even extravagant. When we find we are down to Fig Newtons and canned corn, it is time to go shopping or stop cruising.

We replaced the original stove on our Balboa with a non-pressurized Swedish osmosis model, because there is less chance of burning fuel spewing out of the stove. Whenever possible, we use the propane grill in the cockpit rather than the galley stove, if for no other reason than to avoid lingering cooking odors in the cabin. Our water tank holds only 20 gallons, but on extended cruises, we add another 10-gallon container and store it on the foredeck with shock cords. We use lake or salt water to wash our dishes and reserve our onboard water for rinsing.

Clothing: We try to bring everything we think we may need for the climate in our cruising venue, especially foulies. When we pack, we don't count on being able to do laundry, especially if we are cruising in a remote area. We also bring clothespins for safely hanging up wet towels and clothing. We pack our gear in soft bags, because they take up less space, and we put our towels and linens in plastic boxes or sacks. We also bring extra bags for dirty laundry.

Fuel storage: We carry two vented 2.5-gallon fuel tanks in an aft cockpit locker on the port side, next to the 6.5-gallon main tank and the 6-gallon spare. The main tank and auxiliary tank are vented directly to a dorade vent, with two additional vents for ventilation of the entire area. All fuel tanks stored below are in direct contact with the bottom of the hull or transom, which helps them remain cool.

For longer trips, we may secure another 6-gallon tank on the foredeck. When we make a cruising plan, we carefully estimate how much fuel we will need to cover the distance we plan to travel. For example, our 9.9-horsepower Honda burns approximately 1 gallon of gas every hour at 6 knots. Since we carry a total of 17.5 gallons of gasoline, we have a cruising range of approximately 105 nautical miles. If we plan to go farther, we strap an additional tank to the forward stanchion. I like to provide for the return trip too, particularly if I am not sure about the chances to refuel somewhere along the way and can't count on sufficient and favorable wind.

Of course, the calculation changes dramatically if there is a good breeze. When Jeanine and I cruised the California coast, we covered more than 350 miles and burned less than 12 gallons of fuel. We also carry two fire extinguishers, one mounted on the bulkhead forward of the V-berth and the other aft. We make sure that all flares, safety equipment, and life jackets are easily accessible and that they are in working order.

Miscellaneous gear: Because sails take up a lot of valuable room, we bring only the ones that we think we will need, depending on the wind strengths we expect. But we also have a total of five bags of sails, including a set of tanbarks for heavy weather. For light air we bring a light 180-percent overlapping genoa.

We always carry four anchors. The 18-pound Danforth, which is the primary anchor, is mounted on a pulpit bracket at the bow and secured with shock cords. It is attached to 10 feet of ⁵⁄₁₆-inch chain and 300 feet of ⅜-inch triple-strand nylon rode located in the chain locker. Our second anchor, a 20-pound plow anchor, is secured to 10 feet of chain on 250 feet of ⅜-inch triple-strand nylon line. This one is stored in a cockpit locker in a plastic container on top of the flaked anchor line. The third and fourth anchors with their rodes are also stored aft in separate plastic containers.

We always carry a first-aid kit and ginger ale, ginger snaps, or one of the popular over-the-counter remedies for motion sickness, in case one of our guests suffers from *mal de mer*. We also carry two or three flashlights, extra batteries, extra line, extra matches, and a waterproof plastic box—a ditch bag of sorts, in case we have to abandon ship. The emergency gear includes blankets, cushions, parachute and smoke flares, wooden plugs, and the like.

We also pack a versatile tool kit and special tools, spare fuses, lights, or fittings we think we may need. These tools include wire cutters to sever the shrouds, in case the mast breaks, goes by the board and threatens to punch a hole in the hull. There's also a rubber mallet, socket wrenches for changing spark plugs, extra spark plugs, an extra starter cord for the outboard, and an assortment of large and small wrenches and screwdrivers.

Before casting off, we always double-check what we have packed, but inevitably we later find out that we have forgotten something. If it's not a mission-critical piece of gear or equipment, we figure out how to get along without it. It's one of the enjoyable challenges of learning how to become a prudent trailer sailor.

Appendix IV

Tips for Towing

Securing the boat: A good road trip starts with a boat that is properly secured to the trailer. As veteran trailer boaters know, a good set of tie-down system with straps, hooks, ratchets and buckles makes short work of a difficult job. Forget fumbling with old lines that go slack when they're wet or knots that seize up when the line shrinks in hot, dry weather. Instead, use tie-downs at the stern, at the gunwale and at the bow. As an added safety measure, don't use the trailer winch to secure the bow, but a dedicated tie-down that's attached to the bow's eye. To secure the stern and prevent the boat from bouncing off the trailer, use heavy straps. Tie-downs also spread loads over a wider area and won't roll or slide like ropes can.

If you operate your vessel in saltwater, use tie-downs that are made from nylon or polypropylene webbing with stainless-steel hardware, not the budget version, which has zinc-plated hardware. If your trailer was custom-built for

Make sure that the coupler latch is secure, check the condition of your safety chains and top off the brake fuel reservoir before hooking the trailer to the towing vehicle

your boat, attachment points will be in the right places. Otherwise you might have to improvise and use attachment points on the boat and string the tie-downs to a strong point on the trailer frame, which you can create with U-bolts or brackets. Avoid chafe points and sharp edges by inserting pads for protection.

Secure gear inside the boat, so loose items won't turn into missiles that shoot forward when you step on the brake, possibly piercing a bulkhead or doing other preventable damage to the interior. If you are by yourself and have to clamber all over the boat, cinching up a tie-down can turn into a frustrating exercise if the S-hooks slip out of their place. Relief comes from so-called S-hook keepers that prevent this from happening. These little widgets also are a smart choice for preventing the trailer's safety chain from jumping out of the attachment eyes on the hitch.

Loose rigging should be tied tightly to the mast with shock cord. Many cruisers don't bother with releasing the tension of their diamond wires when unstepping the mast for transport. Racers, on the other hand, are more inclined to do this and they mark the setting of their turnbuckles so when they rig their boats before launching, they have a point of reference. Make sure nothing rubs against a gelcoat or wooden surface of the boat and be generous with protective covers and pads.

Before leaving, check the lights for proper functionality and make sure that the trailer hitch is locked and tight. Don't forget to hook up and secure the safety chain. It's the only device that can save you from catastrophe if the trailer becomes unhitched. Whenever you stop for gas, make it a habit to check all fluids and the air pressure in the tires, and then walk around the rig to make sure all tie-downs are still tight. If your boat has a swing keel, make sure to minimize weight and stress on the hull by releasing the keel so that it rests on the trailer carriage. A word about tires: Keep them properly inflated to avoid expansion and contraction, which is one of the factors that most often contributes to ruined tires. Don't forget to check the spare tire for pressure and keep it out of the sun, either in a protective cover or by storing it inside the trailer box (if you have one).

Trailer permits: A boat with an overall length of 20 or 25 feet might be small on the water, but load it on a trailer and the perspective changes quickly. On the road, that's considered big and might require a special permit for over-wide loads to be trailered on U.S. highways or freeways. The requirements vary from state to state, but eight feet and six inches seems to be the magic number, so check the applicable laws by logging on to the Department of Transportation's Website(s) in the respective state(s) you plan to visit or drive through. In Colorado, the DOT stipulates that "The total outside width of any vehicle or load shall not exceed 102" (2.59 meters), excluding mirrors or safety devices. C.R.S. 42-4-502 (1), (5)" www.dot.state.co.us/truckpermits/lcvfyis.pdf.

City driving: If passing through a city is unavoidable, the key tactic is to drive defensively and to be alert. Watch for bicycles, pedestrians, pets, and kids who might stray into your path and be circumspect when you approach obstructions and intersections that are potentially dangerous. Even when traffic flows, you have to be ready to stop at any time, so keep your distance from the car ahead. Remember, stopping a rig with a heavy trailer load takes three times the distance you'd need when driving unattached. Traffic can suddenly back up or stop without warning, your lane may suddenly merge with another, someone may cut you off, or a truck or bus may swerve into your lane. Ask your co-pilot to read signs, point out intersections, and check maps. If you like 21st-century gadgets, you probably have a GPS with voice command to guide you through the city maze, but as comfortable as that is, it does not absolve you from keeping a sharp lookout.

If you have to turn, follow the rule that is used by professional truck drivers. When you make a right turn, use your turn signal way before you come up on the turn, so the rest of the world is informed about your intentions. Stay wide until your trailer wheels are close to the 90-degree angle made by the curb, then turn, *but look over your right shoulder* for bicyclists and other traffic that might materialize from your dead spot. When making a left turn, be conservative in estimating the speed of oncoming traffic, usually it moves faster than you think. Remember that your rig won't accelerate like an Indy car with a trailer on the hitch and that it is more than twice as long than the towing vehicle alone. Start the actual turn when the trailer wheels approach the center of the intersection and make sure you turn into the right-hand lane if you're entering a road with more than one lane in one direction.

Highway driving: Avoid unnecessary lane changes and watch for stopped traffic ahead or lanes that end or are closed for construction. Professional truck drivers are trained to look ahead to the point where they will be in 12 to 15 seconds, and you should do the same. Maintain an interval of three or four seconds to the vehicle in front of you, instead of the common two-second margin for single cars and light trucks. Barred any other speed limits or conditions that dictate a slower rate of progress, stick to a maximum speed of 65 miles per hour, which will get you there and won't overtax your rig and the load you're towing. Remember that a 15-inch automobile wheel is doing fewer revolutions at any speed than smaller trailer wheels, which means the trailer tires and bearings are much hotter and subject to much more strain. Never tow a boat in overdrive because the gearing is not designed for pulling a load.

Blacktop can become very hot in the summer, which means that tires will be hot too, so much so that even the smallest pinhole in the tire wall could cause a blowout. Stay away from the pieces of shredded tires in your lane. Truckers in the southwest call them "alligators," which is fitting, because they can bite, meaning they are potent hazards for your vehicle or trailer tires.

Cattle and deer: In the western states where open country is common, grazing cattle pose a special problem, because they move in groups along the side of the road where the grass seems to be, well, greener. If one bovine decides to cross, others are likely to follow. Usually they don't do that until you are close enough for an emergency brake maneuver. At night, cattle are difficult or nearly impossible to see, which is why driving on a two-lane road through cattle country after dark can be dangerous. Deer whistles mounted in tandem on a front bumper may spook wayward animals, but they won't necessarily scare them off the road. Instead animals might freeze and stare into a vehicle's headlights, just like Elliott the buck did in the movie *Open Season* when his nemesis Shaw approached in his truck. If you are headed for a collision with an animal, consider it the lesser evil than performing a rash evasive maneuver, which could make you lose control and cause your rig to veer off the road, or worse, into oncoming traffic.

I have found that an Interstate bypass is often a good alternative route to follow, even though it may involve driving extra miles. But there are exceptions to the rule. In Seattle, for example, the Interstate bypass east of Lake Washington is nearly as crowded as Interstate 5, which goes through the heart of the city.

Pace yourself: "Are we there, yet?" Who hasn't heard the whining of the kids in the back of the car? Truth is that we *all* want to get there fast. Time is money, or at least part of the precious vacation. But for safety's sake, a well-timed break (and a loss of a couple of hours) beats a busted boat, the hospital bed, or doing time six feet under. For good reasons the law requires that professional drivers limit their driving time to 10 to 12 hours in a 24-hour period. That's a good guidance for amateurs, too. Don't wait until you nod off for a second, but act on the first signs of fatigue. Pull over, take a nap, or at the very least, let your co-pilot have a turn at the wheel.

Driving in the dark: Assuming that you are a responsible individual who won't leave home without properly working trailer lights, you must also think about the necessity of others to be able to see you. Always turn on the headlights when visibility is reduced in rain or at dusk. Driving in marginal conditions with parking lights is not sufficient and might even be illegal. One important detail is often overlooked: Vehicles that tow a heavy trailer with a considerable tongue weight often end up blinding oncoming traffic, because their headlights are adjusted for normal operation. Unless your vehicle has adjustable headlights, have a mechanic lower the beam before you leave. If oncoming cars flash their bright lights at you, you know you're blinding these drivers, which compromises their ability to see you and makes it very difficult for them to gauge a turn, or judge the distance of oncoming traffic.

Never look directly into an oncoming vehicle's lights. I make it a habit to look slightly to the right of the approaching vehicle, toward the right shoulder. I concentrate on that point until the vehicle has passed. But even so, it can take several seconds for me to regain proper vision.

181

Driving hills: Altitude affects engine efficiency, and your vehicle incurs a loss of power of approximately three or four percent for every 1,000 feet of elevation—that's roughly 40 percent for a 10,000-foot mountain pass such as we have in Colorado. Remember this if you are trying to maintain speed or when passing another vehicle. If you can't keep up with the speed of the rest of the traffic, get into the right lane and turn on your flashers. In many states, it is illegal to hold up more than five vehicles, so if you find that you are an obstacle to traffic flow by frequently checking your rearview mirror, pull over at a turnout or the earliest suitable opportunity and let those behind you pass. Never direct traffic around your rig. If a passing car gets in an accident, you will be held responsible.

In extreme heat or when driving up a steep hill, turn off your air conditioner, which saps considerable power from your engine. Luckily, there is a trade-off between summer heat and mountain roads: The higher you climb, the cooler it gets. A transmission that is run at high speed in the lower gears can heat up quickly. But it is also true that engines overheat if the radiator doesn't get enough cool air, e.g. when plodding up a long hill at a snail's pace. In any case, we always carry an extra container of water for the radiator in case of overheating.

Never pour anything directly on an overheated engine because it can split the block. Leave the engine running and pour the water over (not into) the radiator and into (not over) the reserve tank to reduce the water temperature in the radiator slowly and safely. If you're caught behind a slower vehicle and decide to pass, shift down, put on the left turn signal, and get around the vehicle as quickly as possible. Never pass more than one vehicle at a time and remember that objects in the right-side rearview mirror are "always closer than they appear," so look over your right shoulder when merging back into the right lane.

Going downhill, use your gears and engine as much as possible—not the brakes—to control your speed. Overused brakes are hot and prone to fading. If the road is too steep for the engine's lowest gear to slow you down sufficiently, depress the brake pedal at regular intervals to gradually slow down until you're driving five miles slower than you intended. This may take up to 25 seconds, but when you reach that point, take your foot off the brake pedal and use the lower gears to maintain a safe speed.

Backing and parking: Backing a trailer is one of the quintessential skills for anyone who loves trailer sailing and launches the boat at a ramp. Luckily it's not rocket science, at least when you understand the principle. Practice in an empty parking lot before you embarrass yourself at the launch ramp. If you are new at a launch site, watch how others negotiate the ramp and pick up some tricks. How far do the others have to back down the ramp to let the boats float off? Is it a flat ramp that requires an extension of the trailer tongue so the trailer can go far enough in to make the boat float off? Waiting for a little while has another positive side effect: It allows the wheel bearings to cool down. If they are hot when they hit cold water and they don't have a protective cap, the grease might leak, or the momentary vacuum can suck in water, which compromises the grease. If left untreated, that's a sure-fire recipe for a busted bearing on the next trip. If you must immerse your wheel hubs when ramp launching, use bearing protectors, which keep the grease under pressure and the water out. These protectors also make

Launching is easiest with a small engine if you stay as close as possible to the dock

lubrication much easier, which is an important incentive to keep up routine maintenance.

When backing with a trailer, begin by placing one hand at the bottom of the steering wheel. Now, when you move your hand to the left, turning the front wheels of the tow vehicle to the right, the trailer will turn left and vice versa. Of course, this neat little trick might be moot if you don't have power steering. Always back slowly, so you can adjust for positioning errors. Do not rely on mirrors, but turn around in your seat, so you can see boat and trailer through the rear window. Insurance data indicates that a primary cause of accidents is the failure of an operator to turn around while backing.

Have your mate check behind the trailer to make sure that no one is in or about to enter its path. Be especially alert if children are present because they may dart in front, or worse, into the area behind your trailer without warning. Always keep your trailer in view. If no boat is on it, adjust your seat so you can see the runners or bunks on the trailer bed. They are your guides to position the trailer properly when you back in to haul out.

Parking: Some marinas and launch sites don't allow a vehicle and trailer to be left overnight. If you are planning a longer cruise, consider leaving your vehicle and trailer in a well-lit long-term public or private storage lot. But make sure you can legally park for an extended period when you leave the vehicle and trailer, and carefully read the regulations.

Other safety tips: Never carry extra cans of fuel in the tow vehicle because a rear-end collision that pushes the trailer hard into the back of your vehicle could start a fire. Have a fire extinguisher installed in an accessible place inside the tow vehicle. On the highway, be alert to approaching buses and trucks, because they often create a heavy backwash. If you're not prepared for that blast, it could be enough to make you swerve all over. Constantly check both side and rearview mirrors. Always use turn signals before changing lanes and stay on the defensive. Before leaving, check the trailer lights (the wiring harness should be on your list of annual maintenance items). If you spent some money on a good trailer, your tail-light assembly is removable. Even if it isn't, there are now LED lights that have taken the automotive industry by storm and are about to do the same in the boating world. They are waterproof, dirt and shock resistant and they don't heat up like incandescent bulbs. But if you are still using 19th-century technology, unplug the lights and let them cool for a little while before launching, because cold water can and will blow out the hot bulbs.

One final thought: If there is any question about the road ahead or the weather forecast, treat the trip like a cruise. Assess the potential risk to your boat, your vehicle and your passengers, just as you would when you are contemplating the weather before leaving safe harbor. Once I had the urge to go sailing after a snowfall late in October. Although the roads were clear at the time, it was highly likely that I'd encounter ice on the way back. Although I was tempted, my wife made realize that the risk of losing our boat in a wreck simply wasn't worth a weekend of fun.

Appendix V

Shaking Down the Trailer

The care and maintenance of your trailer does two things: First, it reduces the likelihood of sitting at the side of the road, possibly in the middle of nowhere, trying to effect repairs or improvise to get to a mechanic's shop in the next town when you could be already sailing. Second, knowing your trailer is in good condition is important for peace of mind, for your own safety and that of others. A boat trailer has a number of critical parts, so let's take a look at the basics, which include checking ball, hitch, brakes tires, bearings, brake pads, electrical connections, frame and the boat bunks.

Trailer ball, hitch, and brakes: Like tying down the boat properly, connecting and securing the trailer to the tow vehicle is a fundamental task before you turn the key in the ignition. Sounds obvious, right? Surprisingly, not to everyone. Check the nut under your trailer ball and tighten it, if necessary. Load stress and vibrations are an inevitable part of towing and can cause the nut to work loose. Some balls have a cotter pin to lock the nut, but it still is a good idea to keep on top of it. While you are at it, clean the ball and coat it with fresh grease. If your ball is screwed to your bumper, make sure that your trailer's gross and tongue weights are well within the specified limits, which are usually printed on the bumper or receiver hitch. Most often the limits are around 500 pounds for the tongue weight and 5,000 pounds for the load. If you have a receiver hitch, it will probably be listed at 500 to 1,000 pounds for the tongue and 10,000 pounds for the load.

It is important to position the boat on the trailer properly to achieve the correct tongue weight. If it's too far forward, the tongue weight increases and presses down on the rear axle of the towing vehicle. This lifts the front wheels, so they have less grip, which could make steering difficult and cause the drive wheels to spin if your vehicle has a front-wheel drive. It also causes the headlights to point skywards and blind oncoming traffic. On the other hand, if the boat is too far back on the trailer, the tongue has a tendency to lift, which will take weight off the rear wheels of the towing vehicle. This could result in fishtailing and a loss of control when descending steep hills. From time to time, check the U-joints on the towing vehicle's undercarriage and replace them if you begin to notice vibration.

If you are curious (and you should be) about the exact gross weight of vehicle and towing load, stop at the truck scales. My experience is that they are quite happy to help you weigh your rig. Or you can try a commercial establishment that sells bulk commodities by weight. Quarries, waste recycling facilities, or lumberyards have truck scales. If you are not certain of the towing capacity of your vehicle, check with the manufacturer, an authorized dealer, or mechanic. It's about horsepower, axle and gear ratios. Sometimes this information is posted on a sticker inside your vehicle, either in the glove compartment or on the door on the driver's side. Good axle ratios for towing, meaning the difference between the pinion and the ring gears, can range from 3.2: 1 to 4.1: 1.

Incidentally, if you are towing a relatively heavy keelboat, a truck with a long wheelbase and an 8-foot bed is the way to go. It tracks more smoothly and requires fewer corrections than a towing vehicle with a normal wheelbase. There is a trade-off, of course, because a long wheelbase doesn't turn as easily, so parking and backing up will be a bit more difficult. As a rule of thumb, the gross weight of the towing vehicle should match or exceed the gross weight of boat and trailer. If your towing vehicle is a little bit lighter than the load you are towing, you can shift the balance in favor of the vehicle by stowing as much gear as possible in the vehicle.

The size of the hitch ball is engraved on the top so it is fairly easy to determine if it fits the trailer's coupler. Inspect frequently the coupler latch, the A-frame ball clamp, spring, and lock lever. If they are bent, worn or rusted, they should be replaced, which is no big deal, since auto part stores sell the entire unit. Also make sure that all nuts, bolts, and pins on the receiver hitch are secure and ascertain the tight fit of the U-bolt for your safety chains. Never leave for any trip, long or short, without hooking up the safety chain, by crossing the ends under the hitch and hooking them into the hitch platform. If the trailer jumps off the hitch, the tongue will drop but the trailer remains connected to the vehicle.

If the GVWR (gross vehicle weight rating), the amount of weight that can be carried on the axles of a trailer, exceeds 3,000 pounds, trailer brakes are mandatory in most states. If you have any doubts about the condition of your brake shoes, retractor springs, or slave cylinders, ask a specialist to inspect and replace them if necessary. You should only do this job at home if you have some experience installing and adjusting brakes. Remember, however, that this is a vital safety item, so don't take any chances and have it done by a certified mechanic. If your trailer has surge brakes, make sure that all nuts and bolts connecting the surge actuator to the trailer tongue are tight. Check the master cylinder for water and top it off with brake fluid whenever necessary. If the brake fluid is a milky brown, you might have a leak somewhere. In this case consult with a brake specialist who will know how to trace it. The actuator has a shock absorber that should be inspected to ensure it still has adequate resistance during quick stops. If it feels soft or shows signs of leaks, replace it.

Tires, bearings, and brake pads: The load limits for your tires are printed on the sidewall, so the trailer weight must fall within these limits. To avoid complications from soft tires or unevenly inflated tires, make it a habit to check the pressure with a gauge before you hit the road and, if necessary, stop at a gas station to top off the air to the PSI limit indicated on the tire's sidewall. Again, don't forget the spare. All of your tires should be the same make, type, size and tread. Unlike your car's tires, trailer tires will need to be replaced before the treads are worn out, mainly because of UV damage to the sidewalls while the trailer is in storage. Often, a simple plywood board leaned against the fender while the trailer is not in use, suffices to keep the tires in the shade, which extends their useful life. Blemishes on the sidewalls and treads indicate weak spots in the tire casing and can precipitate a blowout, as we learned first hand on a trip across the desert in southern Idaho.

When you are satisfied with the condition of your tires, don't lean back, but inspect wheel hubs, brakes and bearings and pay special attention to bearing seals and dust caps as you look for leaks. If you suspect a problem or the mere possibility of a problem developing down the line, replace them. To re-grease the bearings, remove the entire wheel from the spindle and apply marine-grade grease by massaging the lubricant into the ball bearings by hand. However, do not over-grease the bearing, because when the bearings get hot at high speed this could build tremendous pressure and blow out your seals. If you have bearing buddies, your bearings *should* be well greased, but that's far from guaranteed, so check and re-lube them if necessary. Buddies or not, do not let the bearings or spindle run dry, since this is the fastest way to ruin both. At the end of this job, tighten the spindle nut until the wheel stops to wobble, then loosen it a quarter turn, lock it with a new cotter pin, and replace the dust cap. Your trailer probably has far fewer miles than your car, so it is likely that the brake pads will be in reasonably good condition. Exceptions are old trailers that have covered many miles, or have sat unused for a long time or trailers that were/are immersed in salt water.

Electrical connections: Most of the problems with electric connections result from corrosion, especially if you operate your boat on the ocean. Make sure the wires are not chafed, especially where they pass through the trailer frame. Look at the connections and the lights and address any corrosion or accumulation of dirt. If necessary, replace them or clean them with an electric cleaner and apply a dab of petroleum jelly to protect them from corrosion. A trailer's lights, connections, and sockets can easily deteriorate in a single season, so remove all bulbs to make sure that the connections have not rusted and there is a solid contact between the bulb and socket. Corrosion is an ever-present possibility, especially in saltwater environments, so it is important to rinse boat and trailer with fresh water as soon as possible.

Alternatively, you can throw some money at the problem and replace the soon-to-be obsolete incandescent bulbs with a set of LED lights. It isn't cheap, but there are several good reasons to do it, including a life expectancy of 100,000 hours, which might be enough to outlive your trailer. LED lights have no filaments that break and no bulb bases to short or corrode and they have a permanent seal in a welded polycarbonate lens, so they are better suited for contact with water and dirt. There's no danger of thermal shock, because LEDs don't generate heat and their low power draw minimizes the chances for a voltage drop.

Bunk and frame: Frequently inspect the condition of your bunk boards, brackets, and guide boards and examine them for cracks or splits. Make sure they are securely bolted to the trailer frame. Don't neglect the nuts and bolts on the bunk frame supports, and tighten the bolts on your keel board guides if necessary, because they tend to work loose with vibration. Next time you launch your boat, look over the bunk carpets and have extra pieces plus some tacks handy to replace old and worn pads. A word of friendly advice regarding your license plate: it's the unloved stepchild of trailer boaters, because it is the first thing that gets dented and bent when the trailer is backed into a fence post or some other hard obstacle. So save yourself from getting pulled over by making sure the license plate light is working and the plate itself is properly aligned and bolted to the trailer frame.

If this seems like a lot of work to you, try to remember that not everything goes bad at the same time. If you keep on top of these basics, you will catch problems before they become a nuisance or before they draw the attention of a highway patrol officer. Most of the routine maintenance can be completed during a simple walkabout at the beginning of the boating season and items that require your attention more frequently can be addressed once or twice a year. In either case, inspection and proactive, preventive maintenance assure a better margin of safety for you, your rig and others, so it is time well spent. Not to mention a smooth trip to and from the sailing venue, so you get the most from your precious vacations.

Appendix VI

Small and Safe

The first rule of sailing is safety, no matter whether you cross an ocean, head down the coast or go sailing on your local reservoir. Safety is right up there with fun, and one should not get neglected at the expense of the other. Safety starts with respect for the water, the weather, the crew and other vessels. Experienced sailors know their limits and that taking unnecessary risks can jeopardize their own safety and that of fellow boaters.

Fire: Of all the onboard emergencies, fire is the most terrifying and dangerous. You must act quickly and decisively and keep your emotions in check. Keep at least two fire extinguishers aboard and place them near potential fire hazards (i.e. the engine compartment and the galley) but not so close that you can't reach them in a case of emergency. First, try to put out the fire without endangering yourself. The first few seconds are the most important, because once a hull catches on fire, it will be almost impossible to extinguish, and you will have to abandon ship. Consider what kind of flammables you have on board and make sure to buy a fire extinguisher that's filled with the right agent. If there has been an explosion, you may only have time to get yourself and your crew over the side. If you can, send a Mayday from the boat's VHF or the handheld backup radio. First save the crew and yourself by getting into the dinghy or by deploying the life raft. Don't forget to grab the abandon-ship bag (see below), then communicate your position so rescuers can find you. If this happens within sight of land or on a lake, the smoke from the fire will attract considerable attention. Once in the dinghy or life raft, update the Mayday with your current condition and position if you're not already in contact with rescue personnel. It all sounds a bit scary, but if you have gone over the procedure of an abandon-ship drill with your crew, everyone will know what to do.

Taking on water: If you hit a hard object (e.g. by grounding) or a hard object hits you (e.g. another vessel) and your boat is taking on water, you should be able to launch an emergency drill to save the boat. Again, time is of the essence, so preparation and communication are important. If you still have power, make sure the electric bilge pump is working at peak capacity. In addition, put someone on the manual bilge pump immediately. If there was no grounding or collision and you see water rising over the floorboards, a thru-hull fitting might be the culprit. Luckily small trailerable yachts have very few of them, so finding the leak should not be difficult. The first order is to reduce the amount of water the boat takes on and to give the pumps a chance to get ahead. So try plugging the hole from the inside. Nearly anything can be used for this: towels, sail cloth, sponges, wooden plugs can be driven into a failing seacock, and larger holes can be patched and braced with battens, paddles, or the lid of the cooler. Pulling a sail or a leak cloth over the damaged area from the outside also can help to slow water ingress. There are several types of sealing compounds, which can be used on a wet surface and will harden under water in a matter of minutes. You might also want to carry an assortment of wooden plugs, which can be bought at just about any marina store. Alert the authorities via radio, but don't wait for someone to come and take you in tow. Head for shore under your own power, if possible. This may be the one time when you will look forward to a grounding.

Collisions: In highly trafficked venues on lakes and along the coast (e.g. the harbor entrance of a busy port like Long Beach), you will always encounter other vessels and with them the possibility of a collision. Assuming the other operator doesn't have any idea of the rules of the road will actually improve your chances of avoiding an incident. If the other vessel is the give-way vessel but doesn't act like it, alter your course early and obviously, slow down, or stop until the situation is clarified. It's better to act too soon than too late. To gauge the course of other boats in your vicinity, use a hand-bearing compass and take a series of bearings on nearby boats to see if they are on a collision course with you. If the bearing holds constant, you and the other vessel are about to collide. Alternatively, you can also point an arm at a boat that seems to be headed your way. Do that twice, 15 seconds apart. If you're still pointing in the exact same direction, you and the other guy are on collision course. At night, the relative bearing of other vessels is even more important, because judging the other's course and distance based on the color of the running lights is very risky. Of course, radar would be helpful here, but not too many trailerable sailboats are equipped with it.

Fog: Radar also would be the silver bullet in fog, but if you don't have it, the least you can do is making sure others can pick up the signal that bounces off your boat. Most of us have experienced a bit of fog-induced claustrophobia at one time or another, and no one welcomes the prospect of cruising in the middle of a dense cloud and trying to make sense of indeterminate sounds that can't be tracked or identified. If caught in this situation (as it can happen in cold-water venues like Maine or San Francisco Bay on any good summer day), hoist your radar reflector and reduce speed. Strictly speaking, only vessels longer than 39 feet are required to sound fog signals, but as a small boat, you want to make your presence known. Blow the horn for one long blast once every two minutes if you are motoring, or give one long blast followed by two short ones if you are sailing. Keep your GPS turned on, so you know where you are and if you're motoring, shut off the engine periodically to hear what is nearby, such as the sound of surf, echoes from the shore, and other boats. The best way to deal with fog, of course, is to stay at your mooring or dock. Remember that only the sailor with no schedule always has good weather. Decisions that are driven by concerns for safety and seamanship, not by schedules, are the most prudent and will keep stress at bay.

Crew safety and the weather: Make sure that your crew masters the basic tasks, such as reefing or dousing the sails, starting the engine, steering the boat when motoring and operating the radio. The storage location of life jackets on board is as important as knowing how to put them on properly. This point is moot if you have inflatable PFDs that are comfortable and must be worn to count as PFDs. Make sure that there is always a proper lookout on deck while under way, fair weather or foul. Therefore good gear and PFDs for every crewmember are not a luxury, but a necessity. Best to have inflatable PFDs that double as a safety harness, which makes them twice as valuable, especially in bad weather, when everybody on deck must wear life jackets and should be clipped into jacklines (lifelines are not adequate attachment points for tethers). Give each one of your crew something to do in a storm to help them feel in control and mitigate the onset of seasickness.

Medicine: Medical kits now are easy to pick out, because they can be chosen for different types of sailing, days spent at sea and number of crew members. Somebody also figured out that packaging the contents in separate transparent plastic containers makes a lot of practical sense, nearly as much as labeling these packages by the type of injury the content is meant to treat, rather than by the content itself. This takes a lot of guesswork out of first aid, especially on boats that don't have a registered nurse or doctor among the crew. Sunscreen, bug spray, antihistamines and a few different remedies against seasickness (e.g. ginger tablets, wristbands, Bonine, or Stugeron—if you can get it) also should be part of your medical arsenal.

Trip planning: Give yourself a margin of safety by planning a route that has good harbors of refuge. Minimize stress by keeping a sane itinerary. Less is more, meaning that covering a distance of 15 to 20 miles a day is plenty for a pleasure cruise. If you intend to cross a large, unprotected body of water, but have doubts about the weather or the weather report, don't go. If there is a small craft warning, listen, because they are talking about you. You are a small craft, so stay put. If you are already out on the water and hear a weather-alert on radio, head for the closest refuge and don't be picky. Remember: Any port in a storm. If you're towing a dinghy and the conditions worsen, get it back on board and stow it securely. Dress warmly *before* you get chilled. It is much better to be hot and having to take off clothing than putting on protective gear when you are already shivering because you're wet and cold. If it's in safety's interest to get someplace fast and using the engine to squeeze out an extra knot or two, or because you can steer a more direct course, by all means do it. The goal is to get out of the weather as quickly as possible.

Lightning: Lightning is as dangerous to small sailboats as it is to large ones. The owner's manuals of most trailer boats usually don't talk about grounding, so presume there is none. A heavy-duty set of jumper cables that are clipped to a stay with the other end hung in the water can help drain high voltage by grounding a lightning strike to the water. If a thunderstorm is bearing down on you, don't touch the mast, the stays, or the chain plates. If you're in a marina, get off the boat.

Anchoring: If you are at anchor and begin to worry about your ground tackle, do something. Don't just sit there and fret. Check the rode, pay out more scope, or set another anchor. Get out the chart and the tide tables, check your position on the GPS, the state of the tide, and the type of bottom. Make sure you are using the right type of anchor for the bottom in your anchorage. If your charts indicate a rocky bottom and you are using a Danforth (which works best in sand and mud), replace or supplement it with a plow or CQR anchor.

Night passages: Be conservative with night sailing, unless you have good charts and/or electronics (GPS, radar) or intimate knowledge of the area. When you decide to stay out after dark, be prepared to deal with commercial traffic and navigational challenges that can be confusing and requires a high degree of alertness and concentration since speed and distance of other vessels are very difficult to gauge. If you think you know your nav lights, don't get too smug. Put your skills to the test on a trip along a densely populated coast on a moonless night, dodging crab pots and steering the boat to the navigation lights, which are very hard to see because of the millions of flashing red lights along the shore. Long Island Sound comes to mind, or the approach of Long Beach Harbor.

The gist: Don't succumb to a false sense of security just because you are planning to cruise within sight of land. If any of your boat's vital gear or safety equipment, including radios, bilge pumps, or rigging, is not up to snuff, fix it before you head out. Repairing anything underway is vastly more difficult than in port. When you take off for your vacation cruise, don't be surprised if you feel some anxiety, which is brought about by a new and unknown venue or challenging conditions or both. We might boast about our adventurous spirit when nothing is at stake, but deep down humans resist change and are wary of new surroundings. You can reduce this anxiety by getting prepared, by studying charts and cruising guides and by talking to people who know the venue before you head out in an effort to learn as much as you can about the nuances of tide and the weather. Realize that the presence of fear or anxiety is not bad, as long as you understand how to manage them. These emotions assure survival, because they focus your attention on problems *and* solutions.

Sailing is a form of recreation that requires courage, stamina, concentration, decision-making and knowledge. It's not for the faint of heart, but it also provides high rewards for problem solving and performing under pressure. Regardless of the circumstances, the way you fare depends on your attitude, so do not engage in negative thinking. Fear often comes from lack of knowledge and the ensuing lack of confidence, so prepare yourself, your crew, and your boat. Knowledge is power, and the more you know, the more comfortable you will feel.

On the road or on the water, prudent trailer sailors have the ability to anticipate the next situation and are prepared to respond deliberately and decisively. They stay one step ahead of the events that are about to unfold. This is what makes them confident and competent.

Bibliography

Lake Powell:

Dowler, Louise Bishop. *Dowler's Lake Powell Boat and Tour Guide*. 1993

Hodgson, Dick. *Brief Cruising Guide to Lake Powell*. Dordt College Press, 1998

Jones, Stan and Steve Waid. *Lake Powell and Its Ninety-Six Canyons: Boating and Exploring Map*

Kelsey, Michael R. *Boater's Guide to Lake Powell*. Michael R. Kelsey Publishing. 1996

Lake Powell Magazine. Adventure Publications, Inc. Sedona AZ (Published spring, summer, and fall—contains detailed maps).

Lake Powell North, Lake Powell South Fish'n'Map Co. www.fishmap.com

Linford, Laurance D. *Navajo Places: History, Legend, Landscape*. Salt Lake City, UT: The University of Utah Press. 2000

Canada and the Pacific Northwest:

Afoot and Afloat Series
Mueller, Marge and Ted. *Middle Puget Sound and Hood Canal* (1997); *North Puget Sound* (2006); *South Puget Sound* (2006); *The San Juan Islands* (1995). Seattle, WA: Mountaineers.

Robert Hale & Co., Inc. *Waggoner Cruising Guide*. Bellevue, WA (published annually).

Scherer, Migael. *A Cruising Guide to Puget Sound and the San Juan Islands, Olympia to Port Angeles*. 2nd edition. Camden ME: International Marine. 2004

California:

Fagan, Brian, *The Cruising Guide to Central and Southern California*. Camden, ME: International Marine. 2002

Griffes, Peter ed. *Pacific Boating Almanac*.

Mexico:

Cunningham, Gerry. *Cruising Guide to the Middle Gulf, Sea of Cortez*.

Cunningham, Gerry. *Sea of Cortez Cruising Charts*

Nobel, John et al. *Mexico: from Copper Canyon to Chichen Itza*. Oakland, CA: Lonely Planet Publications. 2000.

Sea of Cortez North, Sea of Cortez South. Fish'n'Map Co. www.fishmap.com.

Other:

Rousmaniere, John. *The Annapolis Book of Seamanship*. New York: Simon and Schuster, 1989.

Index

Acknowledgements

I would like to thank Lothar Simon and Dieter Loibner of Sheridan House for their support and incisive editorial work in helping me to complete the book and organize it for publication. I would also like to thank the editors of *Sailing, 48 North, Cruising World, Sail* and *Trailer Boating Magazine* for laying the groundwork for the material presented here. Finally, I would like to thank my wife, Jeanine, whose superb advice, editorial savvy, and encouragement have been of immeasurable value in helping me to sharpen the manuscript and prepare it for submission.